THE SIMPLIFIED BALDRIGE AWARD ORGANIZATION ASSESSMENT

Donald C. Fisher, Ph.D.

The Lincoln-Bradley Publishing Group
New York

Permissions Department
The Lincoln-Bradley Publishing Group
305 Madison Avenue – Suite 1166
New York, NY 10165

Publisher's Cataloging in Publication
(Prepared by Quality Books, Inc.)

Fisher, Donald C.
　　The simplified Baldrige Award organization
assessment / Donald C. Fisher.

　　p. cm.
　　Includes bibliographical references.
　　ISBN 1-879111-51-9

　　1. Total quality management – United States –
Handbooks, manuals, etc. 2. Malcolm Baldrige
Quality Award. I. Title.

　　HD62.l5.F57 1993　　　　　　　658.5'62

　　　　　　　　　　　　　　　　　QB192-20055

Printed on approved acid-free paper

Cover Design by Electronic Publishing Services, INC.
Book Design and make-up by Electronic Publishing Services, INC.

1 2 3 4 5 6 7 8 9 10

To my Dad who was my standard of excellence.
With love and appreciation.

PREFACE

This book will help employees conduct a simplified assessment of their organizations based on Baldrige criteria. Many small businesses, not-for-profit organizations and medium to large size manufacturing and service companies have refrained from incorporating Baldrige criteria into their Strategic Planning Processes because of the complexity of the criteria.

The compounded Baldrige criteria questions have been broken down and simplified for easier understanding. The intent is to help employees assess their departments and organizations based on a National Quality Award criteria that can be used as a benchmark against "World-Class" quality organizations.

This book will be of great benefit for any organization's Strategic Planning Process. It is recommended that several employees located at various levels throughout the organization, conduct an organizational assessment. This will allow many sets of eyes to provide input into the Strategic Planning Process.

The author takes liberty in simplifying the questions of the Baldrige criteria. It is with great interest as a member of The Malcolm Baldrige Board of Examiners that this criteria be deployed and used throughout our nation to improve total quality within our organizations.

I would like to thank the Malcolm Baldrige National Quality Award office for allowing me to use excerpts from the Baldrige material for this book. Special thanks are extended to Dr. Curt Riemann, Director of The Baldrige Award and Kathy Leedy, Administrator for the Baldrige Award process, for their cooperation.

TABLE OF CONTENTS

INTRODUCTION ——————————————

BALDRIGE AWARD ORGANIZATION ASSESSMENT

This simplified Baldrige Award Organization Assessment is an excellent tool to provide organizations a basis for Quality Self-Assessment, Strategic Planning, and collecting organizational data to write a Baldrige Award application. This assessment can also be used among various divisions or departments within an organization for internal quality improvement competition.

The Malcolm Baldrige National Quality Award criteria are directed toward delivering improved value to customers while simultaneously maximizing the overall effectiveness and productivity of the organization.

In conducting a Baldrige Assessment of your organization, you will notice that the Baldrige criteria are built upon several Core Values.

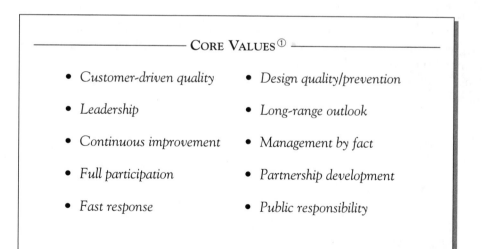

——————————— CORE VALUES[1] ———————————

- *Customer-driven quality*
- *Leadership*
- *Continuous improvement*
- *Full participation*
- *Fast response*

- *Design quality/prevention*
- *Long-range outlook*
- *Management by fact*
- *Partnership development*
- *Public responsibility*

INTRODUCTION

BACKGROUND[2]

As America confronts the realities of the changing global marketplace, the importance of quality to our competitiveness, productivity, and our standard of living has become clear. Stemming from this renewed national quality awareness, Public Law 100-107, the Malcolm Baldrige National Quality Improvement Act of 1987, was signed into law by President Ronald Reagan on August 20, 1987. This Act established the Malcolm Baldrige National Quality Award, named in honor of the former Secretary of Commerce.

The purposes of this Award Program are to:

- Promote quality awareness and practices in U.S. business

- Recognize quality achievements of U.S. companies

- Publicize successful quality strategies and programs

The Malcolm Baldrige National Quality Award Program establishes guidelines and criteria that can be used by organizations in evaluating their own quality improvement efforts. It also provides guidance to American companies by disseminating information detailing how superior organizations were able to change their cultures and achieve eminence. The concept of quality improvement is directly applicable to both small and large manufacturing and service companies. The Malcolm Baldrige National Quality Award encourages quality improvement in all sectors of the economy.

The Secretary of Commerce and National Institute of Standards and Technology are given responsibilities to develop and manage the Award with cooperation and financial support from the private sector. Currently, NIST is working with the American Society for Quality Control, Milwaukee, Wisconsin, to administer the Award.

THE AWARD ②

The Award is traditionally presented by the President of the United States and the Secretary of Commerce at special ceremonies in Washington, D.C.

Awards are made annually to recognize U.S. companies that excel in quality management and quality achievement. As many as two Awards may be given in each of three eligibility categories:

- Manufacturing companies

- Service companies

- Small businesses

Award recipients are expected to share information about their successful quality strategies•with other U.S. organizations.

Basic Eligibility

Public Law 100-107 establishes the three eligibility categories of the Award: Manufacturing, Service, and Small Business. For-profit businesses located in the United States or its territories may apply for the Award. Publicly or privately owned, domestic or foreign-owned, joint ventures, incorporated firms, sole proprietorships, partnerships, and holding companies may apply. Not eligible are local, state, and national government agencies; not-for-profit organizations; trade associations; and professional societies, but these organizations may use the Award criteria for self-improvement in their quest for continuous improvement. Additional information on eligibility is presented in the *1992 Award Criteria*.

Examination Categories

Seven categories are examined in evaluating applicants. A heavy emphasis is placed on quality achievement and quality improvement as demonstrated through the quantitative data furnished by applicants. The seven categories are as follows:

1.0 Leadership

2.0 Information and Analysis

3.0 Strategic Quality Planning

4.0 Human Resource Development and Management

5.0 Management of Process Quality

6.0 Quality and Operational Results

7.0 Customer Focus and Satisfaction

ORGANIZATION OF THE AWARD PROGRAM [2]

Building active partnerships in the private sector, and between the private sector and government, is fundamental to the success of the Award in improving quality in the United States.

Support by the private sector for the Award Program in the form of funds, volunteer efforts, and participation in information transfer is strong and growing rapidly.

The Foundation for the Malcolm Baldrige National Quality Award

The Foundation for the Malcolm Baldrige National Quality Award was created to foster the success of the Program. The Foundation's main objective is to raise funds to permanently endow the Award Program.

Prominent leaders from U.S. companies serve as Foundation Trustees to ensure that the Foundation's objectives are accomplished. Donor organizations vary in size and type and are representative of many kinds of businesses and business groups. To date, the Foundation has raised more than $10.4 million.

National Institute of Standards and Technology (NIST)

Responsibility for the Award is assigned to the Department of Commerce. NIST, an agency of the Department's Technology Administration, manages the Award Program.

NIST's goals are to aid U.S. industry through research and services; to contribute to public health, safety, and the environment; and to support the U.S. scientific and engineering research communities. NIST conducts basic and applied research in the physical sciences and engineering and develops measurement techniques, test methods, and standards. Much of NIST's work relates directly to quality and to quality-related requirements in technology development and technology utilization.

American Society for Quality Control (ASQC)

ASQC assists in administering the Award Program under contract to NIST. ASQC is dedicated to the advancement of the theory and practice of quality control and the allied arts and sciences. ASQC is recognized as a leader in the development, promotion, and application of quality-related information technology for the quality profession, private sector, government, and academia. ASQC recognizes that continuous quality improvement will help the favorable repositioning of American goods and services in the international marketplace.

Board of Overseers

The Board of Overseers is the advisory organization on the Award to the Department of Commerce. The Board of Overseers is appointed by the Secretary of Commerce and consists of distinguished leaders from all sectors of the U.S. economy. The Board evaluates all aspects of the Award Program, including the adequacy of the Criteria and processes for making Awards. An important part of the Board's responsibility is to assess how well the Award is serving the national interest. Accordingly, the Board makes recommendations to the Secretary of Commerce and to the Director of NIST regarding changes and improvements in the Award Program.

Board of Examiners

The Board of Examiners is the body that evaluates Award applications, prepares feedback reports, and makes Award recommendations to the Director of NIST. The Board consists of quality experts primarily from the private sector. Members are selected by NIST through a competitive application process. For 1992, the Board consists of more than 250 members. Of these, 9 serve as Judges, and approximately 50 serve as Senior Examiners. The remainder serve as Examiners. All members of the Board take part in an Examiner Preparation Course.

In addition to their application review responsibilities, Board members contribute significantly to building awareness of the importance of quality and to information transfer activities. Many of these activities involve the hundreds of professional, trade, community and state organizations to which Board members belong.

Award Recipients

The recipients of the Award have shared information on their successful quality strategies with hundreds of thousands of companies, educational institutions, government agencies, health care organizations, and others. By sharing their strategies, Award recipients have made enormous contributions to building awareness of the importance of quality to improving national competitiveness. This sharing has encouraged many other organizations to undertake their own quality improvement efforts.

How to Use the Organization Assessment

The following is a guide to help you complete a thorough assessment of your organization. Explanations are provided for each area.

INFORMATION AND ANALYSIS

2.2b How many different sources of competitive and benchmark data does your organization have?

Notes:

Zero Based Organization

• Comparative data on competition based upon subjective opinion of a few individuals.

• Limited or no benchmarking being conducted.

World Class Organization

• Organization has in place a thorough, on-going search for "Best-in-Class" processes.

40

Area Question
This question takes the Baldrige Criteria and puts it into layman's language. The original Baldrige question appears on the *percent score page* in front of this section.

Notes
Make a note as to where your organization is positioned in response to the question.

Comparisons
Compare your organization with one that is not involved in total quality management (TQM) and another that exceeds TQM. Your organization may fall somewhere in between Zero Based and World Class.

Strengths
Make comments listing organizational strengths.

Areas for Improvement
Make comments listing organizational opportunities for improvement.

Strategic Planning Issues
List strategic planning issues after strengths and areas for improvement are identified.

Short Term Strategies
1 to 2 year TQM plans

Long Term Strategies
3 to 5 year TQM plans

2.2 Competitive Comparisons and Benchmarks

2.2b Current Scope and Uses of Competitive Comparisons and Benchmark Data

+ Strengths

– Areas for Improvement

Strategic Planning Issues:
Short Term –

Long Term –

41

Assessment Comment Guidelines ③

Purpose of Comments

- Basis for your score
- Provides focus on Strategic Planning Issues
- Identifies areas of Strengths and Opportunities for Organizational Improvement

Guidelines for Making Comments

- Comment on each item
- 1 or more comments per item
  typically 2-4 comments
- Make the most important observations
  (+) significant strengths
  (−) significant areas to improve
- Use (+) or (−) notation
  avoid "mixed" comments (+/−)
- Write short, clear sentences — 1 or 2 lines
- Score should be consistent with comments

Comment Examples

+ Excellent integration of human resource improvement strategies with quality requirements and business plans.
− Trends in employee satisfaction indicators were omitted for 1985 and 1986.
+ Organization collects data on all key areas with the majority of their process systems operating in real-time. Customer, supplier and associated data bases are quite good.
+ All customer satisfaction trends show significant improvement over the last 4 years.
− Customer satisfaction data shows organization behind top competitor.
+ Organization uses extensive means to determine customer needs/requirements: focus groups, customer panels, mail and telephone surveys, in-person interviews, etc.
− No mention was made of quality improvement teams in support of organization.

Assessment Scoring System ③

SCORING SYSTEM

The system for scoring Assessment Items is based upon three evaluation dimensions: (1) approach; (2) deployment; and (3) results. All Assessment Items require you to consider these evaluation dimensions before assigning a percent score.

Approach

"Approach" refers to the methods the organization uses to achieve purposes addressed in the Assessment Items. The scoring criteria used to evaluate approaches: include one or more of the following, as appropriate:

- The appropriateness of the methods, tools, and techniques to the requirements
- The effectiveness of the use of methods, tools, and techniques
- The degree to which the approach is systematic, integrated, and consistently applied
- The degree to which the approach embodies effective evaluation/improvement cycles
- The degree to which the approach is based upon quantitative information that is objective and reliable
- The degree to which the approach is prevention-based
- The indicators of unique and innovative approaches, including significant and effective new adaptations of tools and techniques used in other applications or types of businesses

Deployment

"Deployment" refers to the extent to which the approaches are applied to all relevant areas and activities addressed and implied in the Assessment Items. The scoring criteria used to evaluate deployment include one or more of the following, as appropriate:

- The appropriate and effective application by all work units to all processes and activities
- The appropriate and effective application to all product and service features
- The appropriate and effective application to all transactions and interactions with customers, suppliers of goods and services, and the public

Results

"Results" refers to outcomes and effects in achieving the purposes addressed and implied in the Assessment Items. The scoring criteria used to evaluate results include one or more of the following:

- The quality and performance levels demonstrated and their importance
- The rate of quality and performance improvement
- The breadth of quality and performance improvement
- The demonstration of sustained improvement
- The comparison with industry and world leaders
- The organization's ability to show that improvements derive from its quality practices and actions

The percent scores range from a low of 0% for a Zero Based Organization to a high of 100% for a World Class Organization. An organization can be 0% in some areas and 100% (World Class) in others. The Anchor Point is 50% which is a middle range. Many U.S. organizations fall below the 50% Anchor Point. The 50% Anchor Point is considered to be good, but certainly below what an organization that is striving to be the "Best-in-Class" within its industry would score.

MORE ABOUT SCORING

Approach and deployment are considered together. This is done because, without deployment, an approach would merely represent an idea or a plan. The Baldrige Award is based heavily upon "successful quality strategies" which means approaches implemented and deployed.

Anchoring the 50% Point

The 50% point represents a sound approach for accomplishing the principal purposes addressed in the Item. The basic approach should be the way the organization actually operates and should affect most of the people and operations addressed in the Item. The approach should project reasonable confidence that over time there are very likely to be further learning and more complete deployment.

At this level, the main directions of the organization's approach are design and prevention based, but there would nevertheless remain a number of areas where the organization reacts to problems. Such reaction should be used by the organization to improve its systems.

Scoring at 100%

Scoring at 100% should reflect a refined, very mature approach deployed, and well adopted in all relevant areas.

Scoring above 50% (60%-90%)

Scoring above 50% should reflect that learning, refinement, maturity, integration and deployment are taking place. Major weight should be given to *key* areas of deployment. Maturity should be related to learning and refinement over time.

Scoring below 50% (10%-40%)

Scoring below 50% should reflect the beginnings of a systematic approach. Generally, deployment and refinement are not well-defined, and major gaps might exist, particularly at the 10% and 20% levels. Many of the organization's actions are reactive.

Scoring of 0%

Scoring of 0% means that a systematic approach is entirely lacking. In general, there would be no meaningful basis to anticipate how deployment will be achieved. Approach to quality may be entirely or largely reactive.

Scoring Guidelines [1]

SCORE	APPROACH	DEPLOYMENT	RESULTS
0%	• anecdotal, no system evident	• anecdotal	• anecdotal
10-40%	• beginnings of systematic prevention basis	• some to many major areas of business	• some positive trends in the areas deployed
50% Anchor Point	• sound, systematic prevention basis that includes evaluation/improvement cycles • some evidence of integration	• most major areas of business • some support areas	• positive trends in most major areas • some evidence that results are caused by approach
60-90%	• sound, systematic prevention basis with evidence of refinement through evaluation/improvement cycles • good integration	• major areas of business • from some to many support areas	• good to excellent in major areas • positive trends—from some to many support areas • evidence that results are caused by approach
100%	• sound, systematic prevention basis refined through evaluation/improvement cycles • excellent integration	• major areas and support areas • all operations	• excellent (world-class) results in major areas • good to excellent in support areas • sustained results • results clearly caused by approach

INTRODUCTION

HOW TO SCORE YOUR ORGANIZATION

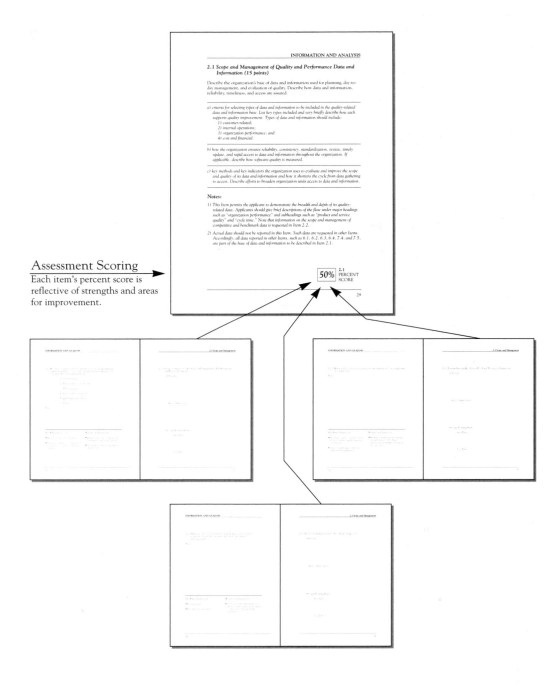

Assessment Scoring
Each item's percent score is
reflective of strengths and areas
for improvement.

ASSESSMENT SCORING

The Assessment is broken down into seven categories which include 1.0 Leadership, 2.0 Information and Analysis, 3.0 Strategy Quality Planning, 4.0 Human Resource Development and Management, 5.0 Management of Process Quality, 6.0 Quality and Operational Results, and 7.0 Customer Focus and Satisfaction. These seven categories are broken into 28 items (i.e. 1.1, 1.2…2.1, 2.2…) and the 28 items are broken down into 89 areas (i.e. a, b,…c…).

The percent score is reflective of the strengths and areas for improvement of the areas within each item. Thus throughout the Assessment all 28 items will obtain a percent score. All item scores will be transferred to the "Summary of Assessment Items" score sheet located in the Conclusion Section.

REFERENCE INFORMATION

For source information, denoted by a numeral in a circle (i.e. ①), please refer to the Conclusion section of this book.

1.0 Leadership

Total section value — 90 points

The *Leadership* Category examines senior executives' personal leadership and involvement in creating and sustaining a customer focus and clear and visible quality values. Also examined is how the quality values are integrated into the company's management system and reflected in the manner in which the company addresses its public responsibilities.

1.1 Senior Executive Leadership (45 points)

Describe the senior executives' leadership, personal involvement, and visibility in developing and maintaining a customer focus and an environment for quality excellence.

---

a) *senior executives' leadership, personal involvement, and visibility in quality-related activities of the company. Include:*
  1) *reinforcing a customer focus*
  2) *creating quality values and setting expectations*
  3) *planning and reviewing programs toward quality and performance objective*
  4) *recognizing employee contributions*
  5) *communicating quality values outside the company*

---

b) *brief summary of the company's quality values and how the values serve as a basis for consistent communication within and outside the company.*

---

c) *personal action of senior executives to regularly demonstrate, communicate, and reinforce the company's customer orientation and quality values through all levels of management and supervision.*

---

d) *how senior executives evaluate and improve the effectiveness of their personal leadership and involvement.*

Notes:

1) *The term "senior executives" refers to the highest ranking official of the organization applying for the award and those reporting directly to that official.*

2) *Activities of senior executives might also include leading and/or receiving training, benchmarking, customer visits, and monitoring other executives, managers, and supervisors.*

3) *Communication outside the company might involve: national, state, and community groups; trade, business, and professional organizations; and education, health care, government, and standards groups. It might also involve the company's stockholders and board of directors.*

1.1
PERCENT
SCORE

1.1a   To what extent are senior executives involved in your organization's quality efforts?

        1. *Goal setting*

        2. *Planning*

        3. *Reviewing organizational quality performance*

        4. *Communicating with employees*

        5. *Recognizing employee contributions*

        6. *Other activities include:*
           – *Learning about quality of domestic and international competitors*
           – *Meeting with customers and suppliers*
           – *Participating in teams*

Notes:

Zero–Based Organization	World–Class Organization
• *Not all senior leaders are personally involved in deploying quality related activities throughout the organization.*	• *Senior leaders are personally and visibly involved in deploying a customer-focused environment for quality excellence throughout the organization.*
• *Senior leaders are not focused on becoming internally customer-driven.*	• *Senior leaders are involved in employee recognition.*

1.1a Senior Executives' Personal Involvement

+ *Strengths*

− *Areas for Improvement*

Strategic Planning Issues:

Short Term −

Long Term −

1.1b   Do senior executives focus and integrate your organization's quality values when they communicate within and outside your organization?

Notes:

Zero–Based Organization

- *Organization's values are not shared with all suppliers and customers.*

- *Organization's values are not shared with new hires during their orientation.*

World–Class Organization

- *Organization has published a values statement.*

- *Organization bases quality values on a corporate quality creed, code of business conduct and operating principles, corporate strategy for excellence, mission statement and supporting guidelines and standards.*

1.1b Senior Executives' Approach to Building Quality Values Within and Outside
Organization

+ *Strengths*

– *Areas for Improvement*

Strategic Planning Issues:

Short Term –

Long Term –

1.1c   Do senior executives communicate your organization's customer orientation and quality values to all levels of management and supervision?

Notes:

Zero–Based Organization	World–Class Organization
• *Executive staff does not communicate quality values throughout the organization in a consistent manner.*	• *President or CEO communicates the organization's customer service orientation and quality values through articles in the employee newsletter, organizational marketing material, and internal/external speeches.*

1.1c Senior Executives' Communication of Quality Values Throughout Organization

+ *Strengths*

– *Areas for Improvement*

Strategic Planning Issues:

Short Term –

Long Term –

1.1d   How do senior executives evaluate and improve their leadership effectiveness and personal involvement within your organization?

Notes:

Zero–Based Organization

- *Senior leaders' personal improvement is not reflected in employee surveys.*

- *Senior leaders have not designed or utilized an evaluation process for their personal leadership involvement.*

World–Class Organization

- *Direct reports rate managers annually with a leadership questionnaire.*

- *Annual employee satisfaction survey is conducted by a third party.*

1.1d Evaluation of Quality Values

　　　+ *Strengths*

　　　– *Areas for Improvement*

　　Strategic Planning Issues:

　　　Short Term –

　　　Long Term –

1.2 Management for Quality (25 points)

Describe how the organization's customer focus and quality values are integrated into day-to-day leadership, management, and supervision of all organizational units.

---

a) *how the organization's customer focus and quality values are translated into requirements for all levels of management and supervision. Include principal roles and responsibilities of each level:*
    1) within their units
    2) cooperation with other units.

---

b) *how the organization's organizational structure is analyzed to ensure that it most effectively and efficiently serves the accomplishment of the organization's customer, quality, innovation, and cycle time objectives. Describe indicators, benchmarks, or other bases for evaluating and improving organizational structure.*

---

c) *types, frequency, and content of reviews of organization and work unit quality plans and performance. Describe types of actions taken to assist units which are not performing according to plan.*

---

d) *key methods and key indicators the organization uses to evaluate and improve awareness and integration of quality values at all levels of management and supervision.*

1.2
PERCENT
SCORE

1.2a   Does your organization hold everyone accountable for quality and do you have specific measures and guidelines for them based on their level, function, and position?

Notes:

Zero–Based Organization

- *Organization's customer focus and quality values are not fully deployed below senior leader level.*

World–Class Organization

- *Organization supports employee participation among all employee levels.*

- *Annual performance reviews reinforce employee involvement and quality levels.*

1.2a   Approaches for Involving Leadership

+ *Strengths*

– *Areas for Improvement*

Strategic Planning Issues:

Short Term –

Long Term –

1.2b Are the various functions or departments within your organization structured to ensure effective and efficient customer service? How do you base your evaluation?

Notes:

Zero–Based Organization

- *Competitive benchmarks are not being conducted for evaluating and improving customer service.*

- *No indications exist that organization is improving in customer service areas.*

World–Class Organization

- *Organization has in place customer service training for customer contact employees.*

- *Benchmarks are conducted to investigate cycle-time reduction in the customer service area.*

1.2b Evaluation and Improvement of Organizational Structure

   + Strengths

   – Areas for Improvement

   Strategic Planning Issues:

      Short Term –

      Long Term –

1.2c Do your employees have regularly scheduled, frequent meetings during which quality of work (reduction of errors) is reviewed against your organization's plans or goals?

Notes:

Zero–Based Organization	World–Class Organization
• *Employees are not involved in identifying quality issues and developing strategies.*	• *Team quality review meetings are held weekly and monthly with formal agendas.*
	• *Review teams are composed of cross-functional members who review daily non-conformers.*

1.2c   Review Process

+ *Strengths*

– *Areas for Improvement*

Strategic Planning Issues:

Short Term –

Long Term –

1.2d Does your organization evaluate the awareness and integration of quality values at all levels? Are the results of this evaluation used to implement changes in your organization's leadership approach to achieve better results?

Notes:

Zero–Based Organization	World–Class Organization
• *Senior management involvement in total quality throughout the organization does not exist.*	• *CEO or President has luncheons with various employee groups.* • *Employee team involvement is widespread throughout the organization.*

1.2d Key Indicators of Effectiveness of Quality Integration

+ *Strengths*

− *Areas for Improvement*

Strategic Planning Issues:

Short Term −

Long Term −

1.3 Public Responsibility (20 points)

Describe how the organization includes its responsibilities to the public for health, safety, environmental protection, and ethical business practices in its quality policies and improvement activities, and how it provides leadership in external groups.

---

a) *how the organization includes its public responsibilities, such as business ethics, public health and safety, environmental protection, and waste management in its quality policies and practices. For each area relevant and important to the organization's business, briefly summarize:*
   1) *how potential risks are identified, analyzed, and minimized*
   2) *principal quality improvement goals and how they are set*
   3) *principal improvement methods*
   4) *principal quality indicators used in each area*
   5) *how and how often progress is reviewed*

---

b) *how the organization promotes quality awareness and sharing with external groups.*

Notes:

1) *Health, safety, environmental, and waste management issues addressed in this Item are those associated with the organization's operations. Such issues that arise in connection with the use of products and services or disposal of products are addressed in Item 5.1.*

2) *Health and safety of employees are not covered in this Item. These are addressed in Item 4.5.*

3) *Trends in indicators of quality improvement in 1.3a should be reported in Item 6.2.*

4) *External groups may include those listed in Item 1.1, Note 3.*

1.3
PERCENT
SCORE

1.3a Does your organization address and integrate business ethics, public health and safety, environmental protection, and waste management into your business practices?

Notes:

Zero–Based Organization

- *Organization does not promote employee safety and does not address environmental protection and waste management in their business practices.*

World–Class Organization

- *Organization promotes environmental concerns among employee groups.*

- *Organization leads industry in promoting a safe work environment for employees.*

1.3a   Deployment of Organization's Quality Policies and Practices

   + *Strengths*

   − *Areas for Improvement*

   Strategic Planning Issues:

      Short Term −

      Long Term −

1.3b   Does your organization encourage all levels of employees to spend time giving speeches, tours, and workshops to promote quality to outside organizations? (i.e. PTA, school systems, etc.)

Notes:

Zero–Based Organization

- *Employees do not share customer satisfaction and quality lessons with outside organizations.*

World–Class Organization

- *Various employee levels conduct customer tours within the head facility.*

- *Employees are encouraged to promote quality and become members in local and national organizations.*

1.3b   Promotion of Quality to Outside Organizations

   + *Strengths*

   − *Areas for Improvement*

      Strategic Planning Issues:

         Short Term −

         Long Term −

2.0 INFORMATION AND ANALYSIS

Total section value — 80 points

The *Information and Analysis* Category examines the scope, validity, analysis, management, and use of data and information to drive quality excellence and improve competitive performance. Also examined is the adequacy of the organization's data, information, and analysis system to support improvement of the organization's customer focus, products, services, and internal operations.

2.1 Scope and Management of Quality and Performance Data and Information (15 points)

Describe the organization's base of data and information used for planning, day-to-day management, and evaluation of quality. Describe how data and information, reliability, timeliness, and access are assured.

---

a) criteria for selecting types of data and information to be included in the quality-related data and information base. List key types included and very briefly describe how each supports quality improvement. Types of data and information should include:
   1) customer-related
   2) internal operations
   3) organization performance
   4) cost and financial

---

b) how the organization ensures reliability, consistency, standardization, review, timely update, and rapid access to data and information throughout the organization. If applicable, describe how software quality is measured.

---

c) key methods and key indicators the organization uses to evaluate and improve the scope and quality of its data and information and how it shortens the cycle from data gathering to access. Describe efforts to broaden organizational units access to data and information.

Notes:

1) This Item permits the applicant to demonstrate the breadth and depth of its quality-related data. Applicants should give brief descriptions of the flaw under major headings such as "organizational performance" and subheadings such as "product and service quality" and "cycle time." Note that information on the scope and management of competitive and benchmark data is requested in Item 2.2.

2) Actual data should not be reported in this Item. Such data are requested in other Items. Accordingly, all data reported in other Items, such as 6.1, 6.2, 6.3, 6.4, 7.4, and 7.5, are part of the base of data and information to be described in Item 2.1.

2.1
PERCENT
SCORE

2.1a Within your organization do you measure data that all employees can understand and will that data help them provide better service to your customers? Data by categories include:

    1. *Customer related*

    2. *Internal operations and processes*

    3. *Employee related*

    4. *Safety, health and regulatory*

    5. *Quality performance*

    6. *Supplier*

Notes:

Zero–Based Organization

- *No quality related data is measured.*

- *Data that is measured is not presented in a "user-friendly" format for employees to understand.*

World–Class Organization

- *Quality related data is integrated and distributed throughout the organization.*

- *Data gathering supports organization's quality efforts.*

2.1a   Criteria for Selection of Data Used for Planning, Day-to-Day Management,
        and Evaluation of Quality

   + Strengths

   − Areas for Improvement

   Strategic Planning Issues:

   Short Term −

   Long Term −

2.1b How is valid data, that your organization uses, disseminated to your employees on a timely basis?

Notes:

Zero–Based Organization

- *No process or technology exists to track, monitor or retrieve quality related data for employees.*

- *Data is not disseminated to employees within various departments.*

World–Class Organization

- *Information systems are fully integrated and user-friendly for information exchange and dissemination throughout the organization.*

2.1b   Processes Ensuring Reliability of Data Used Throughout Organization

+ *Strengths*

– *Areas for Improvement*

Strategic Planning Issues:

Short Term –

Long Term –

2.1c How do you evaluate and improve the scope and quality of your data collection? (i.e. shorten the cycle time from data gathering to employee access)

Notes:

Zero–Based Organization

- *No system exists.*

- *No comparative data exists.*

World–Class Organization

- *Continuous improvement methods are utilized to improve the scope and quality of data collection throughout the organization.*

2.1c   Evaluation and Improvement of Data Scope and Quality

+ *Strengths*

– *Areas for Improvement*

Strategic Planning Issues:

Short Term –

Long Term –

2.2 Competitive Comparisons and Benchmarks (25 points)

Describe the organization's approach to selecting data and information for competitive comparisons and world-class benchmarks to support quality and performance planning, evaluation, and improvement.

---

a) *criteria the organization uses for seeking competitive comparisons and benchmarks:*
   1) *key organizational requirements and priorities*
   2) *with whom to compare – within and outside the organization's industry.*

---

b) *current scope, sources, and uses of competitive and benchmark data, including organization and independent testing or evaluation:*
   1) *product and service quality*
   2) *customer satisfaction and other customer data*
   3) *internal operations, including business processes, support services, id employee-related*
   4) *supplier performance*

---

c) *how competitive and benchmark data are used to encourage new ideas and improve understanding of processes.*

---

d) *how the organization evaluates and improves the scope, sources, and uses of competitive and benchmark data.*

2.2
PERCENT
SCORE

2.2a   Does your organization benchmark outside your industry or competitors? How do you select your benchmarks?

Notes:

Zero–Based Organization

- *No competitive benchmarking is conducted.*

- *Competitive comparisons are not maintained and analyzed for forecasting and planning.*

World–Class Organization

- *Plan to benchmark "Best-in-Class" is in effect.*

- *Benchmarks are conducted throughout the organization.*

2.2a   Criteria and Rationale for Competitive Comparisons and Benchmarks

+ *Strengths*

− *Areas for Improvement*

Strategic Planning Issues:

Short Term −

Long Term −

2.2b How many different sources of competitive and benchmark data does your organization have?

Notes:

Zero–Based Organization

- *Comparative data on competition is based upon subjective opinion of a few individuals.*

- *Limited or no benchmarking is conducted.*

World–Class Organization

- *Organization has in place a thorough, on-going search for "Best-in-Class" processes.*

2.2b Current Scope and Uses of Competitive Comparisons and Benchmark Data

   + *Strengths*

   − *Areas for Improvement*

   Strategic Planning Issues:

      Short Term −

      Long Term −

2.2c Does your organization use competive and benchmark data to encourage new ideas?

Notes:

Zero–Based Organization	World–Class Organization
• *Benchmarking process is neither understood nor used.*	• *Continuously looking for "Best-in-Class" processes to benchmark in order to make organization world-class.*

2.2c   Use of Competitive and Benchmark Data to Improve Organization

+ *Strengths*

– *Areas for Improvement*

Strategic Planning Issues:

Short Term –

Long Term –

2.2d How do you evaluate the scope and validity of your competitive benchmark
data? Do you plan to expand this area?

Notes:

Zero–Based Organization	World–Class Organization
• *Organization has no documented plan to evaluate and improve the scope, sources and uses of competitive and benchmark data.*	• *Benchmarking activities are strategically driven from customer satisfaction improvement committees.*
	• *Organization distributes a document that outlines the benchmark process.*

2.2d Evaluation and Improvement of Competitive and Benchmark Data

    + *Strengths*

    – *Areas for Improvement*

    Strategic Planning Issues:

        Short Term –

        Long Term –

2.3 Analysis and Uses of Organization-Level Data (40 points)

Describe how quality and performance-related data and information are analyzed and used to support the organization's overall operational and planning objectives.

---

a) how customer-related data (Category 7.0) are aggregated, analyzed, and translated into actionable information to support:
   1) developing priorities (or prompt solutions to customer-related problems)
   2) determining relationships between the organization's product and service quality performance and key customer indicators, such as customer satisfaction, customer retention, and market share
   3) developing key trends in customer-related performance for review and planning

---

b) how organization operational performance data (Category 6.0) are aggregated, analyzed, and translated into actionable information to support:
   1) developing priorities for short-term improvements in organizational operations including improved cycle time, productivity, and waste reduction
   2) developing key trends in organization operational performance for review and planning

---

c) how key cost, financial, and market data are aggregated, analyzed, and translated into actionable information to support improved customer-related and organization operational performance.

---

d) key methods and key indicators the organization uses to evaluate and improve its analysis. Improvement should address:
   1) how the organization shortens the cycle of analysis and access to results
   2) how organizational analysis strengthens integration of customer, performance, financial, market, and cost data for improved decision making

---

Notes:

1) This Item focuses primarily on analysis for organization-level strategies, decision making, and evaluation. Usually, data for these analysis come from or affect a variety of organization operations. Some other Items in the Criteria involve analysis of specific sets of data for special purposes such as evaluation of training. Such special analysis should be part of the information base of Items 2.1 and 2.3 so that this information can be included in larger, organization-level analysis.

2) Analysis involving cost, financial, and market data vary widely in types of data used and purposes. Examples include: relationships between customer satisfaction and market share; relationships between quality and costs; relationships between quality and revenues and profits; consequences and cost associated with losses of customers and diminished reputation resulting from dissatisfied customers; relationships between customer retention, costs, and profits; priorities for organization resources allocation and action based upon costs and impacts of alternative courses of action; improvements in productivity and resource use; and improvements in asset utilization.

2.3
PERCENT
SCORE

2.3a   Do you systematically analyze all quality data to identify customer trends, problems, and opportunities for improvement? (i.e. survey analysis, ROI, other types of data analysis)

Notes:

Zero–Based Organization	World–Class Organization
• *No steps have been taken to shorten the cycle time for data management and data access activities.*	• *Customer survey data is turned into actionable information.*
• *Customer data analysis is not systematically linked to key quality indicators established within the organization.*	• *Organization uses quality data to drive improvement.*

2.3a   How Customer Data Are Analyzed into Actionable Information to Support
Customer Satisfaction

+ *Strengths*

– *Areas for Improvement*

Strategic Planning Issues:

Short Term –

Long Term –

2.3b Do you evaluate and improve your data analysis processes? (i.e. looking for continuous improvements in organization's approach to short term improvements within operations, improving cycle time, productivity and waste reduction)

Notes:

Zero–Based Organization	World–Class Organization
• *No evidence that a process exists to ensure that quality related data is available horizontally and vertically to all levels and functions within the organization.*	• *Each department focuses on quality indicators (i.e. timeliness, accuracy, communication, competitive performance, and customer satisfaction)*

2.3b   How Operational Performance Data Is Translated

+ *Strengths*

– *Areas for Improvement*

Strategic Planning Issues:

Short Term –

Long Term –

2.3c   Does your organization collect key cost, financial and market data and translate it into actionable information for employees to use to improve customer service and internal performance?

Notes:

Zero–Based Organization	World–Class Organization
• *No evidence exist that organization collects key cost, financial and market data and translates it into information for employees to use to improve customer service and internal performance.*	• *Cost and financial data are summarized for employees on a monthly and quarterly basis. This data analysis allows the organization to maintain the optimal balance at the lowest cost with the highest response to customer requirements.*

2.3c How Financial and Market Data Is Translated into Actionable Information to Support Organization's Customer and Operational Performance

+ *Strengths*

– *Areas for Improvement*

Strategic Planning Issues:

Short Term –

Long Term –

2.3d How does your organization shorten access and improve the internal data you receive?

Notes:

Zero–Based Organization	World–Class Organization
• *No evidence exists that organization shortens access nor improves data analysis.*	• *Organization uses all data to support and improve performance measurement, performance improvement planning, and problem identification resolution.*
	• *Accessibility of data is continuously reviewed for improvement throughout the organization.*

2.3d   Key Indicators Used to Evaluate and Improve Data Analysis

+ *Strengths*

– *Areas for Improvement*

Strategic Planning Issues:

Short Term –

Long Term –

3.0 STRATEGIC QUALITY PLANNING

Total section value — 60 points

The *Strategic Quality Planning* Category examines the organization's planning process and how all key quality requirements are integrated into overall business planning. Also examined are the organization's short- and longer-term plans and how quality and performance requirements are deployed to all work units.

3.1 Strategic Quality and Organizational Performance Planning Process (35 points)

Describe the organization's strategic planning process for the short term (1-2 years) and longer term (3 years or more) for quality and customer satisfaction leadership. Include how this process integrates quality and organization performance requirements and how plans are deployed.

---

a) *how the organization develops plans and strategies for the short term and longer term. Describe data and analysis results used in developing business plans and priorities, and how they consider:*
  1) *customer requirements and the expected evolution of these requirements*
  2) *projections of the competitive environment*
  3) *risks: financial, market, and societal*
  4) *organization capabilities, including research and development to address key new requirements or technology leadership opportunity*
  5) *supplier capabilities*

---

b) *how plans are implemented. Describe:*
  1) *the method the organization uses to deploy overall plan requirements to all work units and to suppliers, and how it ensures alignment of work unit activities*
  2) *how resources are committed to meet the plan requirements*

---

c) *how the organization evaluates and improves its planning process, including improvements in:*
  1) *determining organization quality and overall performance requirements*
  2) *deployment of requirements to work units*
  3) *input from all levels of the organization*

Note:

Review of performance relative to plans is addressed in Item 1.2.

3.1
PERCENT
SCORE

3.1a   How is your overall business planning process integrated with individual and departmental planning and goal setting for the short term and the longer term?

Notes:

Zero–Based Organization

- *No evidence exists that organization develops long term strategic plans.*

World–Class Organization

- *Customers are involved in the strategic planning process for both short term and long term planning.*

3.1a How Plans and Strategies Are Developed

+ *Strengths*

– *Areas for Improvement*

Strategic Planning Issues:

Short Term –

Long Term –

3.1b   How is your organization's overall quality planning process implemented throughout your organization, to suppliers, and to customers?

Notes:

Zero–Based Organization	World–Class Organization
• *Appears organization does not include employees and suppliers in the strategic planning process.*	• *Each functional unit throughout the organization develops goals to support short and long term objectives.*

3.1b   How Plans Are Implemented

+ *Strengths*

– *Areas for Improvement*

Strategic Planning Issues:

Short Term –

Long Term –

3.1c   Is your organization's strategic planning process reviewed on a continuous basis?

Notes:

Zero–Based Organization

- *Plans bear little or no relation to actions taken by the work force. (Plans are not followed or reviewed by employee groups throughout the organization)*

World–Class Organization

- *Each department reviews plans around organization's strategic plan.*

3.1c   How Strategic Plans and Goals Are Evaluated and Reviewed

+ *Strengths*

– *Areas for Improvement*

Strategic Planning Issues:

Short Term –

Long Term –

3.2 Quality and Performance Plans (25 points)

Summarize the organization's quality and performance plans and goals for the short term (1-2 years) and the longer term (3 years or more).

---

a) for the organization's chosen directions, including planned products and service, markets, or market niches, summarize:
    1) key quality factors and quality requirements to achieve leadership
    2) key organization performance requirements

---

b) outline of the organization's principal short-term quality and organization performance plans and goals:
    1) summary of key requirements and key performance indicators deployed to work units and suppliers
    2) resources committed for key requirements such as capital equipment, facilities, education and training, and personnel

---

c) principal longer-term quality and organization performance plans and goals, including key requirements and how they will be addressed.

---

d) two-to-five year projection of significant improvements using the most important quality and organizational performance indicators. Describe how quality and organizational performance might be expected to compare with competitors and key benchmarks over this time period. Briefly explain the comparison.

3.2
PERCENT
SCORE

3.2a Does your organization have major quality improvement goals and strategies? (List them)

Notes:

Zero–Based Organization

- *No evidence exists that short and long term quality goals are established by the organization.*

World–Class Organization

- *Both short and long term quality goals are fully integrated into the organization's leadership objectives.*

3.2a   Major Quality and Performance Goals and Strategies

+ *Strengths*

– *Areas for Improvement*

Strategic Planning Issues:

Short Term –

Long Term –

3.2b Summarize your organization's short-term (annual) goals and explain how these goals are deployed to both employees and suppliers? What resources are committed to achieve these goals?

Notes:

Zero–Based Organization

- *Short term goals are not shared beyond the senior management level.*

- *Suppliers are not informed of their involvement within the short-term plan.*

World–Class Organization

- *Short-term plans are deployed to individual departments throughout the organization.*

3.2b   Principal Short-Term Quality Plans and Goals

+ *Strengths*

– *Areas for Improvement*

Strategic Planning Issues:

Short Term –

Long Term –

3.2c   Explain how your organization's long-term goals and requirements relate to improving quality?

Notes:

Zero–Based Organization

- *Long-term strategic planning target dates are not shared throughout the organization.*

- *No long-term plans in existence.*

World–Class Organization

- *Long-term plans are shared with employees at all levels, customers and suppliers.*

3.2c   Principal Long-Term Plans and Goals

+ *Strengths*

– *Areas for Improvement*

Strategic Planning Issues:

Short Term –

Long Term –

3.2d What do you project the benefits to be if your organization actually meets the goals outlined in your long- and short-term business plans? How will this compare with your competition and your key benchmarks?

Notes:

Zero–Based Organization

- *Appears projections are not shared with all employees.*

World–Class Organization

- *Long-term projections have been developed.*

3.2d   Projection of Changes in Quality Levels

+ *Strengths*

– *Areas for Improvement*

Strategic Planning Issues:

Short Term –

Long Term –

4.0 HUMAN RESOURCE ──── DEVELOPMENT AND MANAGEMENT

Total section value — 150 points

The *Human Resource Development and Management* Category examines the key elements of how the organization develops and realizes the full potential of the work force to pursue the organization's quality and performance objectives. Also examined are the organization's efforts to build and maintain an environment for quality excellence conducive to full participation and personal and organizational growth.

4.1 Human Resource Management (20 points)

Describe how the organization's overall human resource development and management plans and practices support its quality and organization performance plans and address all categories and types of employees.

---

a) how human resource plans derive from quality and organization performance plans (Item 3.2). Briefly describe major human resource development initiatives or plans affecting:
  1) education, training, and related skill development
  2) recruitment
  3) involvement
  4) empowerment
  5) recognition. Distinguish between the short-term (1-2 years) and the long-term (3 years or more) plan as appropriate.

---

b) key quality, cycle time, and other performance goals and improvement methods for personnel practices such as recruitment, hiring, personnel actions, and services to employees. Describe key performance indicators used in the improvement of these personnel practices.

---

c) how the organization evaluates and uses all employee-related data to improve the development and effectiveness of the entire work force. Describe how the organization's evaluation and improvement processes address all types of employees.

4.1
PERCENT
SCORE

4.1a   Are your organization's human resource plans driven by the quality goals outlined in your strategic business plan?   (i.e. training, development, hiring, employee involvement, empowerment, and recognition)

Notes:

Zero–Based Organization	World–Class Organization
• *Performance evaluations not written in language to reinforce organization's quality values.*	• *Human resource plans integrated with the division's strategic plan.*
• *Training widely dispersed but not focused for each employee's individual career development within the organization.*	• *Organization reflects a team culture and supports this concept through their employee training programs.*

4.1a   Human Resource Plans

+ *Strengths*

– *Areas for Improvement*

Strategic Planning Issues:

Short Term –

Long Term –

4.1b   Are your organization's human resource strategies and goals related to your organization's overall quality improvement goals? (i.e. hiring, recruitment, personnel actions, employee services)

Notes:

Zero–Based Organization

- *No process in place for recruitment and hiring of new employees that is reflective of organization's quality culture.*

World–Class Organization

- *Organization publishes an employee newsletter that communicates organization's values.*

- *Lower than industry average turnover rate.*

- *Improvement action system in place that allows employee input and ensures management response within a designated amount of time.*

4.1b   Key Quality Goals for Human Resource Management

+ *Strengths*

− *Areas for Improvement*

Strategic Planning Issues:

Short Term −

Long Term −

4.1c Give specific examples of how your organization uses employee-related data to improve human resource management? (i.e. employee selection process, quality of training, employee development)

Notes:

Zero–Based Organization

- *Human resource management appears not to be driven by employee related data.*

World–Class Organization

- *Organization uses an employee satisfaction survey and participative management survey to gauge employee satisfaction.*

4.1c   Analysis and Use of Data to Improve Human Resource Management

+ *Strengths*

– *Areas for Improvement*

Strategic Planning Issues:

Short Term –

Long Term –

4.2 Employee Involvement (40 points)

Describe the means available for all employees to contribute effectively to meeting the organization's quality and performance objectives; summarize trends in involvement.

---

a) *management practices and specific mechanisms the organization uses to promote employee contributions, individually and in groups, to quality and organization performance objectives. Describe how and how quickly the organization gives feedback to contributors.*

---

b) *organization actions to increase employee empowerment, responsibility, and innovation. Briefly summarize principal goals for all categories of employees, based upon the most important requirements for each category.*

---

c) *key methods and key indicators the organization uses to evaluate and improve the extent and effectiveness of involvement of all categories and types of employees.*

---

d) *trends in percent involvement for each category of employee. Use the most important indicator(s) of effective employee involvement for each category.*

Note:

Different involvement goals and indicators may be set for different categories of employees, depending on organizational needs and on the types of responsibilities of each employee category.

4.2
PERCENT
SCORE

4.2a   How does your organization promote employee contributions to quality performance objectives?

Notes:

Zero–Based Organization	World–Class Organization
• *Employee contributions are not encouraged or acknowledged.*	• *Special recognition awards given to individual employees and employee teams.*
	• *President's club award in place to promote employee contributions to organization's quality efforts.*

4.2a   Practices to Promote Employee Involvement

    + *Strengths*

    − *Areas for Improvement*

    Strategic Planning Issues:

        Short Term −

        Long Term −

4.2b Does your organization give all employees the authority or autonomy to solve problems and make decisions within their work areas?

Notes:

Zero–Based Organization	World–Class Organization
• *Organization is bureaucratic with a formal structure that does not encourage employee authority or autonomy.*	• *Employees are empowered to make decisions and use innovation within their work areas.*

4.2b   Principal Goals for Employee Involvement

+ *Strengths*

− *Areas for Improvement*

Strategic Planning Issues:

Short Term −

Long Term −

4.2c   Does your organization evaluate and measure the extent and effectiveness of efforts to increase involvement, empowerment and innovation?

Notes:

Zero–Based Organization

- *Lack of formal and informal testing of the organization's climate to determine the degree of employee involvement and satisfaction.*

World–Class Organization

- *Employee satisfaction results are used to evaluate the extent of employee involvement and to identify impediments to involvement.*

4.2c   Key Indicators Used to Evaluate the Extent and Effectiveness of the Employee
Involvement Processes

+ *Strengths*

– *Areas for Improvement*

Strategic Planning Issues:

Short Term –

Long Term –

4.2d Does your organization encourage employee involvement and suggestions through a formal improvement suggestion system? If so, do you see an increase/decrease in percent of employees involved?

Notes:

Zero–Based Organization	World–Class Organization
• *No system in place to gauge employee involvement.*	• *Organization encourages, tracks, and measures employee involvement and suggestions system-wide.*

4.2d   Trends and Current Levels of Involvement by All Employees

+ *Strengths*

− *Areas for Improvement*

Strategic Planning Issues:

Short Term −

Long Term −

4.3 Employee Education and Training (40 points)

Describe how the organization determines what quality and related education and training is needed by employees and how the organization utilizes the knowledge and skills acquired; summarize the types of quality and related education and training received by employees in all categories.

---

a) describe:
> *1) how the organization determines needs for the types and amounts of quality and related education and training to be received by all categories and types of employees. Address:*
>> *a) relevance of education and training to organizational plans*
>> *b) needs of individual employees*
>> *c) all work units having access to skills in problem analysis, problem solving, and process simplification*
> *2) methods for the delivery of education and training*
> *3) how the organization ensures on-the-job use and reinforcement of knowledge and skills*

---

b) summary and trends in quality and related education and training received by employees. The summary and trends should address:
> *1) quality orientation of new employees*
> *2) percent of employees receiving quality and related education and training in each employee category annually*
> *3) average hours of quality education and training per employee annually*
> *4) percent of current employees who have received quality and related education and training*
> *5) percent of employees who have received education and training in specialized areas such as design quality, statistical, and other quantitative problem-solving methods*

---

c) key methods and key indicators the organization uses to evaluate and improve the effectiveness of its quality and related education and training for all categories and types of employees. Describe how the indicators take into account:
> *1) education and training delivery effectiveness*
> *2) on-the-job performance improvement*
> *3) employee growth*

Note:

Quality and related education and training address the knowledge and skills employees need to meet their objectives as part of the organization's quality and performance plans. This may include quality awareness, leadership, problem-solving, meeting customer requirements, process analysis, process simplification, waste reduction, cycle time reduction, and training that affects employee effectiveness and efficiency.

4.3
PERCENT
SCORE

4.3a Does your organization conduct a systematic needs assessment to determine the specific educational needs of different categories of employees? Are the skills learned in training practiced in the work environment?

Notes:

Zero–Based Organization

- *No evidence that training needs assessment surveys are being conducted.*

World–Class Organization

- *Organization conducts needs assessment surveys periodically.*

4.3a   Assessing Quality Education and Training Needs

+ *Strengths*

– *Areas for Improvement*

Strategic Planning Issues:

Short Term –

Long Term –

4.3b   Does training in the following areas within your organization reflect quality concepts, tools, and techniques? (i.e. preventive thinking, customer focus)

1. *Sales training*

2. *Management development or supervisory training*

3. *Technical training on how to perform specific job tasks*

4. *Product or service knowledge training*

5. *Training to perform administrative duties*

6. *Training to comply with governmental or industry regulations*

7. *General education courses such as business, accounting, engineering, etc.*

8. *Orientation training*

9. *Problem solving training*

Notes:

Zero–Based Organization

- *No quality improvement training provided.*

- *No problem-solving training offered for teams.*

World–Class Organization

- *Training throughout the organization reflects quality values.*

4.3b   Summary and Trends in Quality Education and Training

   + *Strengths*

   − *Areas for Improvement*

   Strategic Planning Issues:

      Short Term −

      Long Term −

4.3c What methods and indicators does your organization use to ensure that clear improvements in both employee behavior and quality improvement in the employee's work areas are being demonstrated through improved education and training interventions?

Notes:

Zero–Based Organization

- *Lack of training follow-up beyond course evaluation.*

- *No evidence that most qualified staff are serving as trainers.*

World–Class Organization

- *After employee training course, questionnaires are distributed to all participants and their managers to gauge behavior and quality improvement within their work areas.*

4.3c   Methods and Indicators Used to Evaluate and Improve Training

+ *Strengths*

– *Areas for Improvement*

Strategic Planning Issues:

Short Term –

Long Term –

4.4 Employee Performance and Recognition (25 points)

Describe how the organization's employee performance, recognition, promotion, competition, reward, and feedback processes support the attainment of the organization's quality and performance objectives.

---

a) *how the organization's performance, recognition, promotion, compensation, reward, and feedback approaches for individuals and groups, including managers, support the organization's quality and performance objectives. Address:*
   1) *how the approaches ensure that quality is reinforced relative to short-term financial considerations*
   2) *how employees contribute to the organization's performance and recognition approaches*

---

b) *trends in reward and recognition, by employee category, for contributions to the organization's quality and performance objectives.*

---

c) *key methods and key indicators the organization uses to evaluate and improve its performance and recognition processes. Describe how the evaluation takes into account cooperation, participation by all categories and types of employees, and employee satisfaction.*

4.4
PERCENT
SCORE

4.4a Does your employee recognition and reward system support your organization's quality improvement goals?

Notes:

Zero–Based Organization	World–Class Organization
• *Quality improvement is neither recognized nor rewarded.*	• *Recognition and reward supports organization's quality improvement goals.*

4.4a   How Recognition Is Reinforced

+ *Strengths*

– *Areas for Improvement*

Strategic Planning Issues:

Short Term –

Long Term –

4.4b Does your organization have statistics on the number, percentage and different types of employees who received recognition awards for quality improvement over the last few years?

Notes:

Zero–Based Organization	World–Class Organization
• *No recognition system in place.*	• *Steady increase and positive trends in formal and informal recognition given to employees linked with increased management emphasis on quality improvement.*

4.4b   Recognition/Reward Trends of Individuals and Groups

+ *Strengths*

– *Areas for Improvement*

Strategic Planning Issues:

Short Term –

Long Term –

4.4c Does your organization evaluate and improve the quality of performance measurement, compensation and recognition programs on a continual basis?

Notes:

Zero–Based Organization

- *No evidence that senior managers use a consistent process to improve their employee recognition programs and that this process is based upon employee input.*

World–Class Organization

- *Employee satisfaction survey conducted annually by a third party.*

- *Employee focus groups conducted by senior managers.*

- *Participative management questionnaires conducted.*

4.4c   Key Indicators for Recognition

+ *Strengths*

− *Areas for Improvement*

Strategic Planning Issues:

Short Term −

Long Term −

4.5 Employee Well-Being and Morale (25 points)

Describe how the organization maintains a work environment conducive to the well-being and growth of all employees; summarize trends and levels in key indicators of well-being and morale.

---

a) *how well-being and morale factors such as health, safety, satisfaction, and ergonomics are included in quality improvement activities. Summarize principal improvement goals, methods, and indicators for each factor relevant and important to the organization's work environment. For accidents and work-related health problems, describe how root causes are determined and how adverse conditions are prevented.*

---

b) *mobility, flexibility, and retraining in job assignments to support employee development and/or to accommodate changes in technology, improved productivity, changes in work processes, or organizational restructuring.*

---

c) *special services, facilities, and opportunities the organization makes available to employees. These might include one or more of the following: counseling, assistance, recreational or cultural, and non-work-related education, and outplacement.*

---

d) *how and how often employee satisfaction is determined.*

---

e) *trends in key indicators of well-being and morale. This should address, as appropriate: satisfaction, safety, absenteeism, turnover, attrition rate for customer-contact personnel, grievances, strikes, and worker compensation. Explain important adverse results, if any. For such adverse results, describe how root causes were determined and corrected, or give current status. Compare results on the most significant indicators with those of industry averages, industry leaders, and other key benchmarks.*

4.5
PERCENT
SCORE

4.5a Does your organization constantly work on projects to improve safety, health, ergonomics, employee morale and job satisfaction? (Give examples)

Notes:

Zero–Based Organization	World–Class Organization
• *No specific department or individual dedicated to employee safety.*	• *Organization has smoke-free environment.*
• *Senior management not aware of employee morale issues.*	• *Personal counseling available for employees.*
	• *Employee wellness program in effect.*
	• *Employee safety and health issues viewed as paramount importance to organization.*

4.5a   Well-Being and Morale in Quality Improvement Activities

+ *Strengths*

– *Areas for Improvement*

Strategic Planning Issues:

Short Term –

Long Term –

4.5b Within your organization are employees allowed to move around to different positions and areas?

Notes:

Zero–Based Organization	World–Class Organization
• *Current training programs that exist to provide employees with job mobility, flexibility and retraining appears to be weak.*	• *Cross-training of employees.* • *Guaranteed retraining for job replacement.* • *Transitional employees (hourly and management) are reassigned, retrained and relocated.* • *Career counseling in place.*

4.5b   Supporting Employee Development

   + *Strengths*

   – *Areas for Improvement*

   Strategic Planning Issues:

   Short Term –

   Long Term –

4.5c Does your organization take a proactive approach in offering special services for employees? (i.e. child care facility, ride share, drug rehabilitation program, literacy program)

Notes:

Zero–Based Organization	World–Class Organization
• *Not evident to what extent the organization provides support services.*	• *Free physicals for all employees.*
• *Support services only available for senior managers.*	• *Organization subsidizes child care for employees.*
	• *Organization has drug rehabilitation program.*
	• *Exercise classes and facilities.*

4.5c   Special Services for Employees

+ *Strengths*

– *Areas for Improvement*

Strategic Planning Issues:

Short Term –

Long Term –

4.5d How does your organization determine employee satisfaction? (i.e. surveys, employee focus groups, etc.)

Notes:

Zero–Based Organization	World–Class Organization
• *Not evident that a process is in place to determine employee satisfaction.*	• *Annual employee satisfaction survey in place.*
	• *Employee focus groups are deployed throughout the organization to discuss and determine employee satisfaction issues.*

4.5d   How Employee Satisfaction Is Determined

+ *Strengths*

– *Areas for Improvement*

Strategic Planning Issues:

Short Term –

Long Term –

4.5e Do you have data to support your organization's steady improvement in safety, absenteeism, turnover, attrition rate of customer-contact personnel, employee satisfaction, grievances, and worker compensation within your industry?

Notes:

Zero–Based Organization	World–Class Organization
• *No benchmarks are conducted to compare organization's employee satisfaction with that of competition.*	• *Employee well-being and morale is integrated into organization's quality process.*
• *Employee well-being not a driving force in organization's strategic plan.*	

4.5e   Trends in Key Indicators of Employee Morale

> + *Strengths*

> – *Areas for Improvement*

Strategic Planning Issues:

> *Short Term* –

> *Long Term* –

5.0 MANAGEMENT OF PROCESS QUALITY

Total section value — 140 points

The *Management of Process Quality* Category examines the systematic processes the organization uses to pursue ever-higher quality and organizational performance. Examined are the key elements of process management, including design, management of process quality for all work units and suppliers, systematic quality improvement, and quality assessment.

5.1 Design and Introduction of Quality Products and Services (40 points)

Describe how new and/or improved products and services are designed and introduced and how processes are designed to meet key product and service quality requirements and organizational performance requirements.

---

a) how designs of products, services, and processes are developed so that:
1. *customer requirements are translated into design requirements*
2. *all quality requirements are addressed early in the overall design process by appropriate organizational units*
3. *designs are coordinated and integrated to include all phases of production and delivery*
4. *a process control plan that involves selecting, setting, and monitoring key process characteristics is developed*

---

b) how designs are reviewed and validated, taking into account key factors:
1. *product and service performance*
2. *process capability and future requirements*
3. *supplier capability and future requirements*

---

c) how the organization evaluates and improves the effectiveness of its design and design processes so that new product and service introductions progressively improve in quality and cycle time.

Notes:

1) Design and introduction may include modification and variance of existing products and services and/or new products and services emerging from research and development.

2) Applicant response should reflect the key requirements of the products and services they deliver. Factors that may need to be considered in design include: health, safety, long-term performance, environment, measurement capability, process capability, maintainability, and supplier capability.

3) Service and manufacturing businesses should interpret products and service requirements to include all product- and service-related requirements at all stages of production, delivery, and use.

5.1
PERCENT
SCORE

5.1a Does your organization employ a systematic approach to gather information about customers' requirements and desires, and then translate that information into product or service characteristics and standards?

Notes:

Zero–Based Organization

- *No process in place to determine customer requirements.*

World–Class Organization

- *Customer surveys used to determine customer requirements.*

- *Customer focus groups conducted with all customer levels.*

5.1a   Customer Requirements to Design Requirements

+ *Strengths*

– *Areas for Improvement*

Strategic Planning Issues:

Short Term –

Long Term –

5.1b Describe the overall process your organization uses to design and test new products and services.

Notes:

Zero–Based Organization

- *No system in place to design and test new products and services.*

- *No refined, documented research approach in all areas to assure consistent quality in design plans and testing before introduction of new products and services.*

World–Class Organization

- *Documented product and service design qualifications and release procedures in place to test new products and services.*

5.1b Review and Validation of Design

> *+ Strengths*

> *— Areas for Improvement*

Strategic Planning Issues:

> *Short Term —*

> *Long Term —*

5.1c   Does your organization systematically evaluate and shorten design processes
for new products or services?

Notes:

Zero–Based Organization

- *No documented procedure for cycle-time reduction in place.*

World–Class Organization

- *Pilots are used for cycle-time reduction.*

- *System in place to reduce introduction time for new products or services.*

5.1c   Evaluation and Improvement of Designs

   + *Strengths*

   – *Areas for Improvement*

   Strategic Planning Issues:

      Short Term –

      Long Term –

5.2 Process Management – Product and Service Production and Delivery Processes (35 points)

Describe how the organization's product and service production and delivery processes are managed so that current quality requirements are met and quality and performance are continuously improved.

---

a) *how the organization maintains the quality of processes in accordance with product and service design requirements. Describe:*
  1) *what is measured and types and frequencies of measurements*
  2) *how out-of-control occurrences are handled, including root cause determination, correction, and verification of corrections*

---

b) *how processes are analyzed and improved to achieve better quality, performance, and cycle time. Describe how the following are considered:*
  1) *process simplification*
  2) *waste reduction*
  3) *process research and testing*
  4) *use of alternative technologies*
  5) *benchmark information*

---

c) *how overall product and service performance data are analyzed, root causes determined, and results translated into process improvements.*

---

d) *how the organization integrates process improvement with day-to-day process management.*
  1) *resetting process characteristics to reflect the improvements*
  2) *verification of improvements*
  3) *ensuring effective use by all appropriate organizational units*

Notes:

1) For manufacturing and service organizations which have specialized measurement requirements, a description of the method for measurement quality assurance should be given. For physical, chemical, and engineering measurements, describe briefly how measurements are made traceable to national standards.

2) The distinction between 5.2b and 5.2c is as follows: 5.2b addresses ongoing improvement activities of the organization; 5.2c addresses performance information related to the use of products and services ("performance in the field"), including customer problems and complaints. Analysis in 5.2c focuses on the process level – root cause and process improvement.

5.2
PERCENT
SCORE

5.2a Does your organization control the processes used to produce and deliver your products and services? How do you handle out-of-control processes?

Notes:

Zero–Based Organization	World–Class Organization
• *No integrated product or service control processes exist.*	• *Rigorous and systematic process for sampling output and ensuring adherence to design plans.*
• *No use of control charts are evident.*	
• *Limited deployment of internal audit, input/output check of products produced and/or services provided.*	

5.2a   Process Control Assurance

   + Strengths

   – Areas for Improvement

   Strategic Planning Issues:

   Short Term –

   Long Term –

5.2b Does your organization employ a systematic method for analyzing the causes of process upsets? (i.e. standardized problem solving steps to solve process upsets)

Notes:

Zero–Based Organization	World–Class Organization
• *Organization does not have written procedures on how to handle out-of-control processes.*	• *Complete documented process procedures are in place throughout the organization.*

5.2b How Processes Are Analyzed and Improved

    + Strengths

    – Areas for Improvement

    Strategic Planning Issues:

        Short Term –

        Long Term –

5.2c   Does your organization use a systematic, planned, and structured evaluation
process that verifies predicted and consistent future results? (i.e. evaluation
process calibrated to ensure consistency)

Notes:

Zero–Based Organization	World–Class Organization
• *No evidence of a documented process that guarantees a consistency of service.*	• *Organization uses a structured evaluation process to ensure consistent products and services.*

5.2c   Translation of Product/Service Data into Process Improvements

+ *Strengths*

– *Areas for Improvement*

Strategic Planning Issues:

Short Term –

Long Term –

5.2d How does your organization integrate process improvement in their
      daily management?

Notes:

Zero–Based Organization

- *No evidence of teams using
  measurements to drive improvements.*

World–Class Organization

- *Improved processes are identified,
  documented, and released in
  organization's training materials
  and incorporated in service
  manual revisions.*

5.2d Integration of Process Improvement with Day-to-Day Process Management

+ *Strengths*

– *Areas for Improvement*

Strategic Planning Issues:

Short Term –

Long Term –

5.3 Process Management – Business Processes and Support Services (30 points)

Describe how the organization's business processes and support services are managed so that current requirements are met and quality and performance are continuously improved.

---

a) *how the organization maintains the quality of the business processes and support services. Describe:*
1) *how key processes are defined based upon customer and/or organizational quality performance requirements*
2) *principal indicators used to measure quality and performance*
3) *how day-to-day quality and performance are determined, including types and frequencies of measurements used*
4) *how out-of-control occurrences are handled, including root cause determination, correction, and verification of corrections*

---

b) *how processes are improved to achieve better quality, performance, and cycle time. Describe how the following are used or considered:*
1) *process performance data*
2) *process and organizational simplification and/or redefinition*
3) *use of alternative technologies*
4) *benchmark information*
5) *information from customers of the business process and support services – inside and outside the organization*
6) *challenge goals*

Notes:

1) *Business processes and support services might include activities and operations involving finance and accounting, software services, sales, marketing, information services, purchasing, personnel, legal services, plant and facilities management, basic research and development, and secretarial and other administrative services.*

2) *The purpose of this Item is to permit applications to highlight separately the quality activities for functions that support the product and service production and delivery processes the applicant addressed in Item 5.2. The support services and business processes included in Item 5.3 depend on the applicant's type of business and quality system. Thus, this selection should be made by the applicant. Together, Items 5.1, 5.2, 5.3, 5.4, and 5.5 should cover all operations, processes, and activities of all work units.*

5.3
PERCENT
SCORE

5.3a How does your organization handle quality control of your daily business processes and support services?

Notes:

Zero–Based Organization

- *Business process and support services are not measured.*

- *No root cause determination is conducted for out-of-control processes in the organization's support areas.*

World–Class Organization

- *Business processes and support services have documented processes.*

- *Out-of-control processes are analyzed by teams using a standardized problem solving process.*

5.3a   Maintance of Business Processes and Support Services

   + *Strengths*

   – *Areas for Improvement*

   Strategic Planning Issues:

      Short Term –

      Long Term –

5.3b   How does your organization identify opportunities for continuous improvement? (i.e. use of competitor benchmark data, systematic analysis of changing market, etc.)

Notes:

Zero–Based Organization

- *No method for verifying process improvements are made.*

World–Class Organization

- *Organization conducts benchmarks on a regular basis to identify opportunities for continuous improvement.*

5.3b   Process Improvement to Achieve Better Quality

+ *Strengths*

– *Areas for Improvement*

Strategic Planning Issues:

Short Term –

Long Term –

5.4 Supplier Quality (20 points)

Describe how the quality of materials, components, and services furnished by other businesses is assured and continuously improved.

---

a) *approaches used to define and communicate the organization's quality requirements to suppliers. Include:*
> 1) *the principal quality requirements for key suppliers*
> 2) *the principal indicators the organization uses to communicate and monitor supplier quality*

---

b) *methods used to assure that the organization's quality requirements are met by suppliers. Describe how the organization's overall performance data are analyzed and relevant information fed back to suppliers.*

---

c) *current strategies and actions to improve the quality and responsiveness (delivery time) of suppliers. These may include: partnerships, training, incentives and recognition, and supplier selection.*

Notes:

1) *The term "supplier" as used here refers to other-organization providers of goods and services. The use of these goods and services may occur at any stage in the production, delivery, and use of the organization's products and services. Thus, suppliers include businesses such as distributors, dealers, and franchises as well as those that provide materials and components.*

2) *Methods may include audits, process reviews, receiving inspection, certification, and rating systems.*

5.4
PERCENT
SCORE

5.4a   Does your organization communicate specific quality requirements to your
most critical suppliers?

Notes:

Zero–Based Organization	World–Class Organization
• *No system in place for supplier partnership or supplier certification.*	• *Organization has formal supplier certification process in place.*
	• *Organization has published quality requirements for all critical suppliers.*

5.4a   Communication of Requirements to Suppliers

   + *Strengths*

   – *Areas for Improvement*

   Strategic Planning Issues:

      Short Term –

      Long Term –

5.4b Does your organization have a well-defined process that ensures
      supplier quality?

Notes:

Zero–Based Organization	World–Class Organization
• *Organization has no process in place to ensure quality requirements are met by suppliers.*	• *Formal process exists that ensures quality standards are met by suppliers.*

5.4b   Methods Used to Ensure Supplier Quality

+ *Strengths*

– *Areas for Improvement*

Strategic Planning Issues:

Short Term –

Long Term –

5.4c Has your organization established a cooperative relationship with key
      suppliers? (i.e. supplier partnerships, supplier award program, supplier
      certification)

Notes:

Zero–Based Organization	World–Class Organization
• *No system for communicating organization's quality requirements to major suppliers.*	• *Organization has a supplier award/recognition system in place.*
	• *Certified supplier program in place.*
	• *Partnerships exist with critical suppliers.*

5.4c   Strategies/Actions to Improve Supplier Quality and Responsiveness

+ *Strengths*

– *Areas for Improvement*

Strategic Planning Issues:

Short Term –

Long Term –

5.5 *Quality Assessment (15 points)*

Describe how the organization assesses the quality and performance of its systems, processes, and practices and the quality of its products and services.

---

a) approaches the organization uses to assess:
> *1) systems, processes, and practices*
> *2) products and services*

> *For 1) and 2), describe: a) what is assessed; b) how often assessments are made and by whom; and c) how measurement quality and adequacy of documentation of processes and practices are assured.*

---

b) how assessment findings are used to improve: products and services, systems, processes, practices, and supplier requirements. Describe how the organization verifies that assessment findings are acted on and that actions are effective.

Notes:

1) The systems, processes, practices, products, and services addressed in this Item pertain to all organization unit activities covered in Items 5.1, 5.2, 5.3, and 5.4. If the approaches and frequency of assessment differ appreciably for different organizational activities, this should be described in this Item.

2) Adequacy of documentation should take into account legal, regulatory, and contractual requirements as well as knowledge preservation and transfer to help support all quality-related efforts.

5.5
PERCENT
SCORE

5.5a Does your organization audit or assess products, services, and the processes used to create them?

Notes:

Zero–Based Organization	World–Class Organization
• *No mature audit process in place.*	• *Products and services are assessed by the use of customer surveys, complaint feedback, warranty data, and market share information.*
• *No evidence that process is in place for making documentation readily accessible to those responsible for design, implementation, assessment, and improvement of processes and quality.*	

5.5a   Approaches Organization Uses to Assess Quality of Products/Services

+ *Strengths*

– *Areas for Improvement*

Strategic Planning Issues:

Short Term –

Long Term –

5.5b Does your organization systematically follow up on its audit findings and
correct audit-detected problems?

Notes:

Zero–Based Organization	World–Class Organization
• *No evidence that process audits are conducted.*	• *Audit findings are deployed to teams throughout the organization to drive continuous improvement.*

5.5b How Assessment Findings Are Used to Improve Products/Services

+ *Strengths*

– *Areas for Improvement*

Strategic Planning Issues:

Short Term –

Long Term –

6.0 QUALITY AND OPERATIONAL RESULTS

Total section value — 180 points

The *Quality and Operational Results* Category examines the organization's quality levels and improvement trends in quality, organization operational performance, and supplier quality. Also examined are current quality and performance levels relative to those of competitors.

6.1 *Product and Service Quality Results (75 points)*

Summarize trends in quality and current quality levels for key product and service features; compare the organization's current quality levels with those of competitors.

---

a) trends and current levels for all key measures of product and service quality.

---

b) current quality level comparisons with principal competitors in the organization's key markets, industry averages, industry leaders, and others as appropriate. Briefly explain bases for comparison such as:

      1) independent surveys, studies, or laboratory testing

      2) benchmarks

      3) organizational evaluations and testing. Describe how objectivity and validity of comparisons are assured

---

Notes:

1) Key product and service measures are measures relative to the set of all important features of the organization's products and services. These measures, taken together, best represent the most important factors that predict customer satisfaction and quality in customer use. Examples include measures of accuracy, reliability, timeliness, performance, behavior, delivery, after-sales services, documentation, and appearance.

2) Results reported in Item 6.1 should reflect the key product and service features in the overview.

3) Data reported in Item 6.1 are intended to be results of organizational ("internal") measurements – not customer satisfaction or other customer data, reported in Items 7.4 and 7.5. If the quality of some key product or service features cannot be determined effectively through internal measures, external data may be used. Examples include data collected by the organization, as in 7.1c, data collected by third party organizations on behalf of the organization, and collected by independent organizations. Such data should provide information on the organization's performance relative to specific product and service features, not on levels of overall satisfaction. These data, collected regularly, are then part of a system for measuring quality, monitoring trends, and improving processes.

6.1
PERCENT
SCORE

6.1a   Does your organization have three years or more of data related to quality improvement of your products and services? (i.e. graphs, historical data showing improvement trends, etc.)

Notes:

Zero–Based Organization	World–Class Organization
• *Not evident that organization is tracking product/service quality during production and after delivery.*	• *Organization tracks product and service quality during production and after delivery.*
• *Limited tracking of product or quality service.*	• *Product/service quality shows positive trends over the past three years.*

6.1a   Trends and Current Levels for Key Measures of Product and
Service Quality

+ *Strengths*

– *Areas for Improvement*

Strategic Planning Issues:

Short Term –

Long Term –

6.1b Specifically how is your organization comparing your quality results with that of your competitors?

Notes:

Zero–Based Organization	World–Class Organization
• *No formal benchmarking being conducted.*	• *Organization conducts competitive benchmarks to compare quality results.*
• *Comparisons to competitors not outlined in plan.*	• *Personnel assigned to collect industry/competitor data.*
• *No consistent access to competitive data. Data collected is anecdotal.*	

6.1b Current Quality Level Comparisons with Principal Competitors

+ *Strengths*

– *Areas for Improvement*

Strategic Planning Issues:

Short Term –

Long Term –

6.2 Organization Operational Results (45 points)

Summarize trends and levels in overall organization operational performance and provide a comparison of this performance with competitors and appropriate benchmarks.

---

a) *trends and current levels for key measures of organization operational performance.*

---

b) *comparison of performance with that of competitors, industry averages, industry leaders, and key benchmarks. Give and briefly explain basis for comparison.*

Note:

Key measures of organization operational performance include those that address productivity, efficiency, and effectiveness. Examples should include generic indicators such as use of manpower, materials, energy, capital, and assets. Trends and levels could address productivity indices, waste reduction, energy efficiency, cycle time reduction, environmental improvement, and other measures of improved overall organizational performance. Also include organization-specific indicators the organization uses to monitor its progress in improving operational performance. Such organization-specific indicators should be defined in tables or charts where trends are presented. Trends in financial indicators, properly labeled, may be included in this Item. If such financial indicators are used, there should be a clear connection to the performance improvement activities of the organization.

6.2
PERCENT
SCORE

6.2a   Does your organization collect data that measures their operational performance? (i.e. productivity indices, waste reduction, cycle time reduction, environmental improvement)

Notes:

Zero–Based Organization	World–Class Organization
• *Organization does not collect data on operational performance.*	• *Organization's business plan provides direction (goals and guidance on collecting data) to drive continuous improvement in operations.*
	• *Trends have been charted over the past three years and deployed throughout the organization.*

6.2a   Trends and Current Levels of Organization's Operational Performance

+ *Strengths*

– *Areas for Improvement*

Strategic Planning Issues:

Short Term –

Long Term –

6.2b   How does your organization's data compare with that of competitors and key benchmarks?

Notes:

Zero–Based Organization

- *Performance measurement data not collected on competitors and industry leaders.*

World–Class Organization

- *Organization collects benchmark data on industry and world leaders.*

6.2b Comparison with Industry and World Leaders

+ *Strengths*

– *Areas for Improvement*

Strategic Planning Issues:

Short Term –

Long Term –

6.3 Business Processes and Support Service Results (25 points)

Summarize trends and current levels in quality and performance improvement for business processes and support services.

a) *trends and current levels for key measures of quality and performance of business processes and support services.*

b) *comparison of performance with appropriately selected companies and benchmarks. Give and briefly explain basis for comparison.*

Note:

Business processes and support services are those as covered in Item 5.3. Key measures of performance should reflect the principal quality, productivity, cycle time, cost, and other effectiveness requirements for business processes and support services. Responses should reflect relevance to the organization's principal quality and organizational performance objective addressed in organizational plans, contributing 6.1 and 6.2. They should also demonstrate broad coverage of organizational business processes, support services, and work units and reflect the most important objectives of each process, service, or work unit.

6.3
PERCENT
SCORE

6.3a Specifically what data does your organization collect that is related to quality improvement within your business processes, operations and support services? (i.e. graphs, historical data showing improvement trends, etc.)

Notes:

Zero–Based Organization	World–Class Organization
• *Limited quality improvement data analyzed in the business process and support service areas.*	• *All business processes and support services have annual quality improvement objectives for data collection.*

6.3a   Trends and Current Levels of Business Processes and Support Services

+ *Strengths*

– *Areas for Improvement*

Strategic Planning Issues:

Short Term –

Long Term –

6.3b Do competitive comparisons demonstrate that your organization is better than industry and world leaders?

Notes:

Zero–Based Organization

- *Organization does not benchmark industry and world leaders.*

World–Class Organization

- *Organization benchmarks "Best-in-Class" processes to compare performance.*

6.3b   Comparison of Performance with Industry and World Leaders

+ *Strengths*

– *Areas for Improvement*

Strategic Planning Issues:

Short Term –

Long Term –

6.4 Supplier Quality Results (35 points)

Summarize trends in quality and current quality levels of suppliers; compare the organization's supplier quality with that of competitors and with key benchmarks.

a) trends and current levels for the most important indicators of supplier quality.

b) comparison of the organization's supplier quality levels with those of competitors and/or with benchmarks. Such comparisons could be industry averages, industry leaders, principal competitors in the organization's key markets, and appropriate benchmarks. Describe the basis for comparisons.

Note:

The results reported in Item 6.4 derive from quality improvement activities described in Item 5.4. Results should be broken down by major groupings of suppliers and reported using the principal quality indicators described in Item 5.4.

6.4
PERCENT
SCORE

6.4a   Does your organization track improvement of your key suppliers?

Notes:

Zero–Based Organization	World–Class Organization
• *Quality audits of suppliers are not performed.*	• *Quality audits of suppliers are performed.*
• *Organization does not have a vender/supplier program plan.*	• *Organization tracks supplier performance.*

6.4a   Supplier Quality Results

   + *Strengths*

   – *Areas for Improvement*

   Strategic Planning Issues:

   Short Term –

   Long Term –

6.4b   How does your key suppliers' quality compare to that of industry competitors and/or to benchmark organizations?

Notes:

Zero–Based Organization	World–Class Organization
• *Organization has no understanding of benchmark process.*	• *Organization conducts supplier quality benchmarks.*

6.4b   Supplier Comparisons with Industry and World Leaders

   + Strengths

   – Areas for Improvement

   Strategic Planning Issues:

      Short Term –

      Long Term –

7.0 CUSTOMER FOCUS AND SATISFACTION

Total section value — 300 points

The *Customer Focus and Satisfaction* Category examines the organization's relationship with customers and its knowledge of customer requirements and of the key quality factors that determine marketplace competitiveness. Also examined are the organization's methods to determine customer satisfaction, current needs and levels of satisfaction, and those results relative to competitors.

7.1 Customer Relationship Management (65 points)

Describe how the organization provides effective management of its relationships with its customers and uses information gained from customers to improve customer relationship management strategies and practices.

---

a) *how the organization determines the most important factors in maintaining and building relationships with customers and develops strategies and plans to address them. Describe these factors and how the strategies take into account: fulfillment of basic customer needs in the relationship; opportunities to enhance the relationship; provision of information to customers to ensure the proper setting of expectations regarding products, services, and relationships; and roles of all customer-contact employees, their technology needs, and their logistics support.*

---

b) *how the organization provides information and easy access to enable customers to seek assistance, to comment, and to complain. Describe types of contact and how easy access is maintained for each type.*

---

c) *follow-up with customers on products, services, and recent transactions to help build relationships and to seek feedback for improvement.*

---

d) how service standards that define reliability, responsiveness, and effectiveness of customer-contact employees' interactions with customers are set. Describe how standards requirements are deployed to other organizational units that support customer-contact employees, how the overall performance of the service standards system is monitored, and how it is improved using customer information.

e) how the organization ensures that formal and informal complaints and feedback received by all organizational units are aggregated for overall evaluation and use throughout the organization. Describe how the organization ensures that complaints and problems are resolved promptly and effectively.

f) how the following are addressed for customer-contact employees:
  1) selection factors
  2) career path
  3) special training to include: knowledge of products and services; listening to customers; soliciting comments from customers; how to anticipate and handle problems or failures ("recovery"); skills in customer retention; and how to manage expectations
  4) empowerment and decision-making
  5) attitude and morale determination
  6) recognition and reward
  7) attrition

g) how the organization evaluates and improves its customer relationship management practices. Describe key indicators used in evaluations and how evaluations lead to improvements, such as in strategy, training, technology, and service standards.

7.1
PERCENT
SCORE

7.1a   How does your organization determine fulfillment of basic customer needs? Do you develop strategies and plans to address them?

Notes:

Zero–Based Organization	World–Class Organization
• *No system, strategy plan or method exists to understand basic customer needs.*	• *Customer advisory board in place.*
	• *Round table executive sessions held with customers.*
	• *Organization conducts exit interviews with customers.*

7.1a How Organization Determines Most Important Factors in Maintaining and Building Customer Relationships

+ *Strengths*

− *Areas for Improvement*

Strategic Planning Issues:

Short Term −

Long Term −

7.1b   How does your organization ensure that customers have easy access to comment on your organization's products or services?

Notes:

Zero–Based Organization	World–Class Organization
• *Customer input is not encouraged.*	• *Customer focus groups in existence.*
	• *President has open door policy for customers.*
	• *1-800 number installed for customer assistance.*

7.1b How Organization Provides Easy Access for Customer Assistance

   + *Strengths*

   – Areas for Improvement

   Strategic Planning Issues:

      Short Term –

      Long Term –

7.1c How frequent, thorough and objective is your organization's follow-up to customers on products, service and transactions?

Notes:

Zero–Based Organization	World–Class Organization
• *No customer follow-up process exists.*	• *Process methodologies developed to analyze customer complaints.*

7.1c Customer Follow-up

+ *Strengths*

– *Areas for Improvement*

Strategic Planning Issues:

Short Term –

Long Term –

7.1d   What does your organization do to develop the service skills of
customer-contact personnel?

Notes:

Zero–Based Organization	World–Class Organization
• *No customer-contact training exists.*	• *Customer-contact personnel are taught state-of-the-art customer service skills.*

7.1d How Customer-Contact Service Standards Are Set

+ *Strengths*

– *Areas for Improvement*

Strategic Planning Issues:

Short Term –

Long Term –

7.1e   How does your organization analyze and use customer complaints
and feedback?

Notes:

Zero–Based Organization	World–Class Organization
• *Organization does not collect formal and informal complaints from customers.*	• *Organization collects all formal and informal customer complaints and feedback and enters them into a data base in their mainframe computer. This data is then distributed to appropriate departments.*

7.1e   How Organization Ensures That All Customer Complaints Are Aggregated
for Overall Evaluation

+ *Strengths*

– *Areas for Improvement*

Strategic Planning Issues:

Short Term –

Long Term –

7.1f How does your organization ensure that employees who have contact with customers are selected properly and given the latest, state-of-the-art tools and technology that your organization can afford?

Notes:

Zero–Based Organization	World–Class Organization
• *Customer-contact is neither rated nor rewarded within the organization.*	• *Customer-contact is considered to be an integral part of the organization.*

7.1f   Selection, Training and Development of Customer-Contact Employees

+ *Strengths*

– *Areas for Improvement*

Strategic Planning Issues:

   Short Term –

   Long Term –

7.1g How does your organization evaluate its performance in managing relationships with customers?

Notes:

Zero–Based Organization	World–Class Organization
• *No formal process exists for improving customer service.*	• *Formal process in place to improve relationships with customers. (i.e. customer service training, published customer service standards, etc.)*

7.1g How Organization Improves Its Customer Relationship
Management Practices

+ *Strengths*

– *Areas for Improvement*

Strategic Planning Issues:

Short Term –

Long Term –

7.2 Commitment to Customers (15 points)

Describe the organization's explicit and implicit commitments to customers regarding its products and services.

---

a) *types of commitments the organization makes to promote trust and confidence in its products, services, and relationships. Describe how these commitments:*
      1) address the principal concerns of customers
      2) are free from conditions that might weaken customer confidence

---

b) *how improvements in the quality of the organization's products and services over the past three years have been translated into stronger commitments. Compare commitments with those of competitors.*

---

c) *how the organization evaluates and improves its commitments, and the customers' understanding of them, to avoid gaps between expectations and delivery.*

Note:

Commitments may include product and service guarantees, product warranties, and other understandings with the customer, expressed or implied.

7.2
PERCENT
SCORE

7.2a How does your organization promote trust and confidence in its products, services, and relationships? (i.e. written warranty, simple understanding of guarantee, etc.)

Notes:

Zero–Based Organization

- *No written warranties/guarantees for products/services issued.*

World–Class Organization

- *Organization issues written warranty/guarantee for all products/services in understandable language.*

7.2a   Types of Commitments

+ *Strengths*

– *Areas for Improvement*

Strategic Planning Issues:

Short Term –

Long Term –

7.2b   Do you have data that supports a trend of continuous improvements in your warranties, guarantees, and other commitments to customers?

Notes:

Zero–Based Organization

- *Organization does not collect data that compares their customers warranties/guarantees with those of competitors.*

World–Class Organization

- *Organization benchmarks others to review how they demonstrate customer commitment.*

- *Organization ensures that all warranties/guarantees are written in an understandable manner for customers.*

7.2b How Improvements in the Quality of Products and Services Are Translated
into Stronger Commitments

+ *Strengths*

– *Areas for Improvement*

Strategic Planning Issues:

Short Term –

Long Term –

7.2c How does your organization evaluate and improve your customers'
understanding of your commitments?

Notes:

Zero–Based Organization

- *No customer survey conducted to gauge customer understanding of commitments.*

World–Class Organization

- *Organization conducts surveys and customer focus meetings (formal and informal) to continually improve its commitments.*

7.2c   How Organization Improves Its Customer Commitments

+ *Strengths*

– *Areas for Improvement*

Strategic Planning Issues:

Short Term –

Long Term –

7.3 *Customer Satisfaction Determination (35 points)*

Describe the organization's methods for determining customer satisfaction and customer satisfaction relative to competitors; describe how these methods are evaluated and improved.

---

a) *how the organization determines customer satisfaction. Include:*
   1) *a brief description of market segments and customer groups and the key customer satisfaction requirements for each segment or group*
   2) *how customer satisfaction measurements capture key information that reflects customers' likely market behavior*
   3) *a brief description of the methods, processes, and sales used; frequency of determination; and how objectivity and validity are assured*

---

b) *how customer satisfaction relative to that for competitors is determined. Describe:*
   1) *organization-based comparative studies*
   2) *comparative studies or evaluations made by independent organizations, including customers*

   For 1) and 2) describe how objectivity and validity are assured.

---

c) *how the organization evaluates and improves its overall process and measurement scales for determining customer satisfaction and customer satisfaction relative to that for competitors. Describe how other indicators (such as gains and losses of customers) and customer dissatisfaction indicators (such as complaints) are used in this improvement process.*

Notes:

1) *Customer satisfaction measurement may include both a numerical rating scale and descriptors assigned to each unit in the scale. An effective customer satisfaction measurement system is one that provides the organization with reliable information about customer views of specific product and service features and the relationship between these views or ratings and the customer's likely market behaviors.*

2) *Indicators of customer dissatisfaction include complaints, claims, refunds, returns, repeat services, litigation, replacements, downgrades, repairs, and warranty costs. If the organization has received any sanctions under regulation or contract during the past three years, include such information in the Item. Briefly summarize how sanctions were resolved or give current status.*

3) *Organization-based or independent organization comparative studies in 7.3b may take into account one or more indicators of customer dissatisfaction.*

7.3
PERCENT
SCORE

7.3a   How does your organization determine customer satisfaction for its different customer groups?

Notes:

Zero–Based Organization

- *No evidence that management regularly reviews customer satisfaction trends and indicators and does not take deliberate actions to change processes to improve customer satisfaction.*

World–Class Organization

- *Organization determines customer satisfaction for its different customer groups through its annual customer survey.*

7.3a   How Organization Determines Customer Satisfaction

+ *Strengths*

– *Areas for Improvement*

Strategic Planning Issues:

Short Term –

Long Term –

7.3b How does your organization's customer satisfaction levels compare to those of your competitors?

Notes:

Zero–Based Organization

- *No data exists to determine customer satisfaction.*

World–Class Organization

- *Customer surveys and customer focus groups are used to collect data relative to competitors.*

7.3b   Determining Customer Satisfaction Relative to Competitors

   + Strengths

   – Areas for Improvement

   Strategic Planning Issues:

   Short Term –

   Long Term –

7.3c How does your organization evaluate and improve its approach to determining customer satisfaction?

Notes:

Zero–Based Organization	World–Class Organization
• *No evidence that evaluation of customer satisfaction process is compared to competitors and industry leaders.*	• *Organization involves customer-contact employees in determining customer satisfaction.*

7.3c Evaluating and Improving Methods for Determining Customer Satisfaction

+ *Strengths*

– *Areas for Improvement*

Strategic Planning Issues:

Short Term –

Long Term –

7.4 Customer Satisfaction Results (75 points)

Summarize trends in the organization's customer satisfaction and trends in key indicators of dissatisfaction.

a) *trends and current levels in indicators of customer satisfaction, segmented as appropriate.*

b) *trends and current levels in indicators of customer dissatisfaction. Address all indicators relevant to the organization's products and services.*

Notes:

1) *Results reported in this Item derive from methods described in Item 7.3 and 7.1c and e.*

2) *Indicators of customer dissatisfaction are listed in Item 7.3, Note 2.*

7.4
PERCENT
SCORE

7.4a   Do you collect data that measures how levels of customer satisfaction has improved over the last several years?

Notes:

Zero–Based Organization	World–Class Organization
• *No data available to determine trends.*	• *Organization shows trend data in comparison to its competitors.*

7.4a   Trends and Current Levels as Indicators of Customer Satisfaction

    + *Strengths*

    – *Areas for Improvement*

    Strategic Planning Issues:

        Short Term –

        Long Term –

7.4b Does your organization measure adverse customer indicators such as complaints, claims, refunds, no call returns, repeat services, litigation, replacements, down grades, warranty costs, and warranty work?

Notes:

Zero–Based Organization	World–Class Organization
• *No documented follow-up methods, disciplines, controls, and processes in place to address adverse customer indicators.*	• *Organization leads competitors and industry leaders in reducing adverse customer indicators.*

7.4b   Trends and Current Levels of Customer Dissatisfaction

+ *Strengths*

− *Areas for Improvement*

Strategic Planning Issues:

Short Term −

Long Term −

7.5 Customer Satisfaction Comparison (75 points)

Compare the organization's customer satisfaction results with those of competitors.

---

a) *trends and current levels in indicators of customer satisfaction relative to that of competitors, based upon methods described in Item 7.3. Segment by customer group, as appropriate.*

---

b) *trends in gaining or losing customers, or customer accounts, to competitors.*

---

c) *trends in gaining or losing market share to competitors.*

Note:

Competitors include domestic and international ones in both the organization's domestic and international markets.

7.5
PERCENT
SCORE

7.5a   Does your organization collect data that measures customer satisfaction with your products and/or services against satisfaction with competitors' products/services?

Notes:

Zero–Based Organization

- *Organization does not collect customer satisfaction data relative to their competition.*

World–Class Organization

- *Competitive comparisons show positive trends.*

- *Organization versus competition shows a positive trend.*

7.5a   Comparison of Customer Satisfaction Relative to Competitors

+ *Strengths*

– *Areas for Improvement*

Strategic Planning Issues:

Short Term –

Long Term –

7.5b   Does your organization measure customer turnover? Do you conduct customer
       exit interviews?

Notes:

Zero–Based Organization

- *Organization does not measure customer turnover.*

World–Class Organization

- *Customer turnover is measured.*

- *Customer exit interviews conducted.*

7.5b   Trends in Gaining or Losing Customers to Competitors

+ *Strengths*

– *Areas for Improvement*

Strategic Planning Issues:

Short Term –

Long Term –

7.5c   Has your organization's market share increased as a result of its quality improvement efforts? (i.e. not because of decreased prices or reduced competition)

Notes:

Zero–Based Organization	World–Class Organization
• *Organization is weak in measuring market share against major competitors.*	• *Market share has increased 10% over the past three years as a result of organization's customer focus.*

7.5c   Trends in Gaining or Losing Market Share Relative to Major Competitors

+ *Strengths*

.

– *Areas for Improvement*

Strategic Planning Issues:

Short Term –

Long Term –

7.6 *Future Requirements and Expectations of Customers (35 points)*

Describe how the organization determines future requirements and expectations of customers.

---

a) *how the organization addresses future requirements and expectations of customers.*
   Describe:
   1) *the time horizon for the determination*
   2) *how data from current customers are projected*
   3) *how customers of competitors and other potential customers are considered*
   4) *how important technological, competitive, societal, economic, and demographic factors and trends that may bear upon customer requirements and expectations are considered*

---

b) *how the organization projects key product and service features and the relative importance of these features to customers and potential customers. Describe how potential market segments and customer groups are considered. Include considerations that address new product/service lines as well as current products and services.*

---

c) *how the organization evaluates and improves its processes for determining future requirements and expectations of customers. Describe how the improvement process considers new market opportunities and extensions of the time horizon for the determination of customer requirements and expectations.*

7.6
PERCENT
SCORE

7.6a How does your organization determine future requirements and expectations of customers? (i.e. customer focus groups, third party surveys, etc.)

Notes:

Zero–Based Organization	World–Class Organization
• *No "end-user" surveys are conducted.*	• *Future requirements and expectations are determined by surveys, focus groups, and benchmark data.*

7.6a   How Organization Addresses Future Requirements and Expectations
of Customers

   + *Strengths*

   – *Areas for Improvement*

   Strategic Planning Issues:

      Short Term –

      Long Term –

7.6b How does your organization determine new product/service lines
for customers?

Notes:

Zero–Based Organization

- *No competitive or industry benchmarking takes place to help determine future product/service features for customers.*

World–Class Organization

- *Cross-functional teams undertake the task of projecting future requirements and expectations of customers.*

7.6b   Determining Future Product/Service Features

+ *Strengths*

− *Areas for Improvement*

Strategic Planning Issues:

Short Term −

Long Term −

7.6c How does your organization evaluate and improve its new product/service line introductions? Follow-up on how satisfied current customers are with your organization's products and services?

Notes:

Zero–Based Organization

- *Organization appears weak in evaluating future customer requirements and expectations.*

World–Class Organization

- *Organization uses customer focus groups and a customer advisory council to address future customer requirements and expectations.*

7.6c How Organization Evaluates and Improves Future Customer Requirements
and Expectations

+ *Strengths*

– *Areas for Improvement*

Strategic Planning Issues:

Short Term –

Long Term –

CONCLUSION

SUMMARY OF EXAMINATION ITEMS	Total Points Possible	Percent Score 0-100% (10% units)	Score (A x B)
	A	**B**	**C**

1.0 LEADERSHIP 90 POSSIBLE POINTS

1.1 Senior Executive Leadership	45	%	
1.2 Management for Quality	25	%	
1.3 Public Responsibility	20	%	
Category Total	90 Sum A		Sum C

2.0 INFORMATION AND ANALYSIS 80 POSSIBLE POINTS

2.1 Scope and Management of Quality and Performance Data and Information	15	%	
2.2 Competitive Comparisons and Benchmarks	25	%	
2.3 Analysis and Uses of Organization-Level Data	40	%	
Category Total	80 Sum A		Sum C

3.0 STRATEGIC QUALITY PLANNING 60 POSSIBLE POINTS

3.1 Strategic Quality and Organization Performance Planning Process	35	%	
3.2 Quality and Performance Plans	25	%	
Category Total	60 Sum A		Sum C

4.0 HUMAN RESOURCE DEVELOPMENT AND MANAGEMENT 150 POSSIBLE POINTS

4.1 Human Resource Management	20	%	
4.2 Employee Involvement	40	%	
4.3 Employee Education and Training	40	%	
4.4 Employee Performance and Recognition	25	%	
4.5 Employee Well-Being and Morale	25	%	
Category Total	150 Sum A		Sum C

SUMMARY OF EXAMINATION ITEMS	Total Points Possible **A**	Percent Score 0-100% (10% units) **B**	Score (A x B) **C**
5.0 MANAGEMENT OF PROCESS QUALITY 140 POSSIBLE POINTS			
5.1 Design and Introduction of Quality Products and Services	40	%	
5.2 Process Management – Product and Service Production and Delivery Processes	35	%	
5.3 Process Management – Business Processes and Support Services	30	%	
5.4 Supplier Quality	20	%	
5.5 Quality Assessment	15	%	
Category Total	140 Sum A		Sum C
6.0 QUALITY AND OPERATIONAL RESULTS 180 POSSIBLE POINTS			
6.1 Product and Service Quality Results	75	%	
6.2 Organization Operational Results	45	%	
6.3 Business Process and Support Service Results	25	%	
6.4 Supplier Quality Results	35	%	
Category Total	180 Sum A		Sum C
7.0 CUSTOMER FOCUS AND SATISFACTION 300 POSSIBLE POINTS			
7.1 Customer Relationship Management	65	%	
7.2 Commitment to Customers	15	%	
7.3 Customer Satisfaction Determination	35	%	
7.4 Customer Satisfaction Results	75	%	
7.5 Customer Satisfaction Comparison	75	%	
7.6 Future Requirements and Expectations of Customers	35	%	
Category Total	300 Sum A		Sum C
GRAND TOTAL (D)	1000		D

HOW TO ORDER COPIES OF THE AWARDS MATERIAL

Note:

The *Award Criteria* and the *Application Forms and Instructions* are two separate documents.

Individual Orders

Individual copies of either document can be obtained free of charge from:

Malcolm Baldrige National Quality Award
National Institute of Standards and Technology
Route 270 and Quince Orchard Road
Administration Building, Room A537
Gaithersburg, MD 20899
Telephone: 301-975-2036
Telefax: 301-948-3716

Bulk Orders

Multiple copies of the *Award Criteria* may be ordered in packets of 10 from:

American Society for Quality Control
Customer Service Department
P.O. Box 3066
Milwaukee, WI 53201-3066
Toll free: 800-952-6587
Telefax: 414-272-1734

Order Item Number T995. Cost: $24.95 per packet of 10 plus postage and handling. Postage and handling charges are:

1 packet	$ 3.50
2-4 packets	5.75
5 or more	11.50

This book, THE SIMPLIFIED BALDRIGE AWARD ORGANIZATION ASSESSMENT, along with related products, may be ordered by contacting:

The Lincoln-Bradley Publishing Group
New York, at (212) 953-1125

Or you may contact:

Creative Living, Inc. • P.O. Box 808 • Gatlinburg, TN 37738
(615) 436-4762   Quantity discounts are available.

Past Award Winners: 1988 to 1992

1992 Award Winners

Manufacturing	Service	Small Business
AT&T Network Systems Group Transmission Systems Business Unit Morristown, NJ	AT&T Universal Card Services Jacksonville, FL	Granite Rock Company Watsonville, CA
Texas Instruments, Inc. Defence Systems & Electronics Group Dallas, TX	The Ritz-Carlson Hotel Company Atlanta, GA	

1991 Award Winners

Manufacturing		Small Business
Solectron Corp. San Jose, CA	Zytec Corp. Eden Prairie, MN	Marlow Industries Dallas, TX

1990 Award Winners

Manufacturing	Service	Small Business
Cadillac Motor Car Company San Jose, CA	Federal Express Corp. Memphis, TN	Wallace Co., Inc. Houston, TX
IBM Rochester Rochester, MN		

1989 Award Winners

Manufacturing	
Milliken & Company Spartanburg, SC	Xerox Business Products and Systems Stamford, CT

1988 Award Winners

Manufacturing		Small Business
Motorola, Inc. Schaumburg, IL	Westinghouse Commercial Nuclear Fuel Division Pittsburgh, PA	Globe Metallurgical, Inc. Cleveland, OH

REFERENCE INFORMATION

The following list consists of source information for the footnotes designated in the Introduction of this book.

① Source: *1992 Award Criteria*, Malcolm Baldrige National Quality Award.

② Source: *1992 Handbook for the Board of Examiners*, Malcolm Baldrige National Quality Award.

③ Source: *1992 Malcolm Baldrige National Quality Award Examiners Course Training Material*, Malcolm Baldrige National Quality Award.

④ Source: *1992 Award Criteria*, Malcolm Baldrige National Quality Award - examination items and notes are excerpted throughout the organization assessment.